SOUTH AFRICA

THE INSIDER'S GUIDE

SOUTH AFRICA

the insider's guide

Ian Michler &

Tessa van Schaik

CONTENTS

AUTHORS' NOTE 7

WELCOME TO SOUTH AFRICA 11
Feature: All that glitters — gold, diamonds
and more 16

TRAVEL SOUTH AFRICA 18
The hot spots 22
World Heritage Sites 22
Tourism offices and websites 25
Planning your trip 26
The gay and lesbian scene 35
Travel with care and caution 35

BE ENTICED 39
Top attractions 41

FROM APARTHEID TO
THE RAINBOW NATION 46
At a glance 49
Fact file: South Africa 49
A brief history 53
Feature: Nobel laureates 62

PLATEAUS AND PLAINS 67
Topography 69
Seven biomes 69
Feature: South Africa's varied topography 70
Climatic patterns 72

EN ROUTE 74
Main national routes 77
Other options 81

CITY TO CITY 82
Cape Town 85
Johannesburg and Soweto 89
Pretoria 92
Durban 94

COUNTRY ROADS 98
Little Karoo 101
Great Karoo 105
Overberg 108
Garden Route 110
Mpumalanga 114

Eastern Free State   117
Kalahari   118
KwaZulu-Natal Midlands   121
The uKhahlamba/Drakensberg range   122
Eastern Cape coast   124
West Coast and Namaqualand   128

ON SAFARI   132
Safari options   135
Feature: Wildlife highlights   136
Fact file: The national parks and
    marine reserves   138
South African National Parks   138
Parks and reserves   139
Feature: The Wilderness Leadership School   142
Feature: Transfrontier Conservation Areas   147
Best of the rest   150
The private reserves   151
Be guided   157

WILDLIFE WONDERS   161
Under threat   175
Science and conservation   177

OUT OF THE WAY   181
IAi-IAis/Richtersveld Transfrontier Park   183
Tswalu Kalahari Reserve   184
Mapungubwe National Park   185

THE LIFE AND SOUL   187
Who's who in South Africa   189
Feature: African independent churches   192
Township life   193
Feature: So to speak   196

TRAVEL ADVISORY   199
Travel basics   200
Directory   204

INDEX   205

*T*his book is dedicated to our son, Liam Theo Michler. He came into our lives during the making of it and has been an absolute joy way beyond our wildest imagination. It is our hope that he will one day be able to roam this continent and experience its natural wonders in the way that we have been so fortunate to have done.

It has been with the invaluable assistance and support of others that we have been able to complete this project. Our thanks and heartfelt gratitude go especially to: Patrick Boddam-Whetham from Wilderness Safaris, Ian Hunter from Hunter Hotels, Valerie Senekal from Conservation Corporation Africa (CC Africa), Richard and Sarah Daugherty from Bhangazi Horse Safaris, Richard and Mouse Poynton from Cleopatra Mountain Farmhouse, Bridget Stephenson from Tswalu Kalahari Reserve, Shayne Richardson-Bayly from Agencies Inc., Ian Taylor from Tinga Private Game Lodge, Nicki Mahony from Isibindi Africa Lodges, Nick and Carol Fox from Sibuya Game Reserve, Alta Coetzee from Die Hantam Huis, Charles Roux from Red Mountain Nature Reserve, Zandri Zaaiman from Ebenaeser Guesthouse, Wynn Green from Millard Mountain Lodge, Dave Martin from Bulungula Lodge, Dalene and Spud Murray from Raptor's View, Charles and Gardi Major from Major Adventures, Vaughn and Chantal Piccione from Berg House and Cottages, Louis de Clercq and Jennifer Schormann from Afri-diziac Tourism Solutions, Baron van der Westhuizen from IAi-IAis/Richtersveld Transfrontier Park, Peppi and Sophia van der Merwe from the Willow Historical Guest House, Lesley-Ann Meyer from Mountain Zebra National Park, Grant Millar from The Haven, Christa Hahn from Drostdy Hotel, Astrid Christianson from Barberton Tourism, and the Lilliput House in Clarens.

Also to Rosie Finlayson for her assistance with translations, Rob Ainslie for his input on the Kgalagadi and Kruger, Angie Bunyard and Johnathan Worby for taking care of us in Mpumalanga, Jeremy Nathan for his chauffeuring skills around Johannesburg, and the great Russell Juds for finding time to shoot our family portrait.

Also to Peter and Beverly Pickford – we are thrilled to be able to boast their work between the pages of this book. For us, they are Africa's leading natural history photographers and right up there with the very best in the world. Also to Iva Spitzer, Robbyn Moir, Michael McMillan, Galeo Saintz, Hunter Hotels and Wilderness Safaris for allowing us use of their fantastic images.

To Felicity Nyikadzino Berold, Roelien Theron and Alana Boligello at Struik Publishers, editor Patricia Myers Smith, designer Peter Bosman and the rest of the production team, thanks for your creativity and hard work.

Ian would like to thank his work colleagues at Invent Africa – Ian McMillan, Robbyn Moir and Ian McCallum – for their patience and understanding. Tessa thanks Jane Spickernell for her unstinting support and keeping their company, The Planet Thing, rolling.

HALF TITLE PAGE *While they are the least common of the large predators, cheetah can still be seen in many parks and reserves, particularly those in the drier regions.*
TITLE PAGE *This woman comes from the Riemvasmaak community near the Orange River in the Northern Cape.*
PREVIOUS PAGES *Low tide at the Keurbooms River mouth, Plettenberg Bay.*
OPPOSITE *The best places to view lions are in the Kruger National Park and the adjoining private reserves of Sabi Sand and Timbavati.*

LEGEND

————	NATIONAL ROAD / MOTORWAY
———	MAIN ROAD
—·—·—	INTERNATIONAL BOUNDARY
———	PROVINCIAL BOUNDARY
◉ PRETORIA	CAPITAL CITY
● CAPE TOWN	PROVINCIAL CAPITAL CITY
● DURBAN	MAJOR CITY
○ Humansdorp	TOWN
Namaqua NP 	PARK AND RESERVE
Crocodile	RIVER
SWAZILAND	COUNTRY NAME
Gauteng	PROVINCIAL NAME
Cape Vidal	CAPE AND PENINSULA

WINDHOEK

NAMIBIA

Kgalagadi Transfrontier NP

Molopo

Molopo

Upington

IAi-IAis / Richtersveld Transfrontier Park

Riemvasmaak

Augrabies Falls NP

Keimoes

Alexander Bay

Vioolsdrif

Onseepkans

Orange

Kakamas

Groblershoo

Pella

Port Nolloth

Steinkopf

Pofadder

Kenhardt

Nababeep Okiep

Goegab NR

Springbok

Namaqua NP

Kamieskroon

Garies

Maryd

Namaqualand

Northern Ca

Brandvlei

Carnarv

Nieuwoudtville

Williston

ATLANTIC OCEAN

Olifants

Calvinia

Vredendal

Vanrhynsdorp

Great Karoo

Fraserburg

Lambert's Bay

Klawer

Tankwa-Karoo NP

Sutherland

Elands Bay

Clanwilliam

Wuppertal

St Helena Bay

Citrusdal

Paternoster

Velddrif

Piketberg

Great Berg

Vredenburg

Porterville

Saldanha

Langebaan

West Coast NP

Malmesbury

Tolbagh

Wellington

Ceres

Touws River

Western Cape

Matjiesfontein

Laingsburg

Ladismith

Swart NR

Calitzdorp

Table Bay

Paarl

Worcester

Montagu

Barrydale

Little Karo

CAPE TOWN

Bellville

Robertson

Bontebok NP

Riversdale

Table Mountain NP

Stellenbosch

Swellendam

Albertinia

Cape of Good Hope

False Bay

Caledon

Riviersonderend

Heidelberg

Napier

Cape Infanta

Hermanus

Bredasdorp

De Hoop NR

Kogelberg Biosphere Reserve

Gansbaai

Arniston

L'Agulhas

Agulhas NP

Cape Agulhas

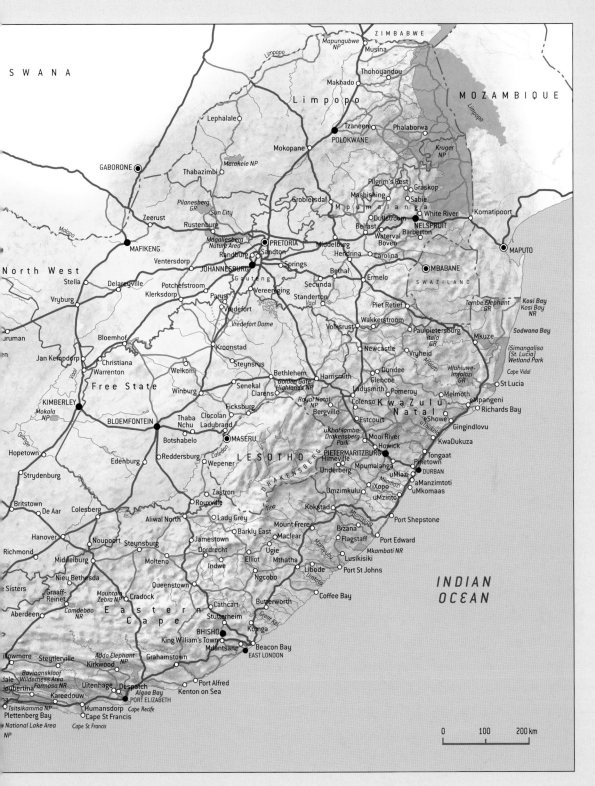

Welcome to
SOUTH AFRICA

PREVIOUS PAGES *A typical sunrise scene in the Great Karoo.*
OPPOSITE *Voters queue outside a polling station in Soweto on 27 April 1994, the day of South Africa's first democratic election.*

ABOVE *These women, grape pickers in the Western Cape, wear a naturally prepared cream for sun protection when working in the fields.*

*O*n the morning of 27 April 1994, more than 19 million South African citizens headed to the polls. Filled with the anticipation and hope that comes with the yearning for a new dawn, they queued for hours on end in urban centres and remote rural areas to cast their votes in what was the first free and fair national election ever held in South Africa. On 10 May, their patience bore fruit when Nelson Mandela was proudly inaugurated as South Africa's first democratically elected president, and the global community welcomed South Africa back into its fold. It's hard to believe that, in this day and age, a country as prominent and as influential as South Africa would only achieve freedom at the very end of the twentieth century. But then, it was in many ways a small wonder that these events took place at all.

During the turbulent years leading up to that election day, a period when almost a century of institutionalised racism was being repealed and replaced with a constitution that would become the envy of the world, many predicted that violence and revenge would be the more likely scenario. Their prediction was based on fact: ever since the Sharpeville shootings in 1960, South Africa had been at war with itself. Tensions and divisions had grown as an increasingly militant black majority attempted to rid South Africa of oppression, while the apartheid government responded with draconian and brutal measures. The riots in Soweto in 1976 gave South Africa's leaders another warning, yet the conflict escalated throughout the 1980s as South Africa seemed to live on the edge of a low-intensity civil war. Fortunately, a massive dose of good sense and bold leadership came next. Although historians and South Africans are divided as to the order in which these occurred, and how to evaluate the reasons and accord the credits, the feared bloody conflict, incredibly, never materialised. Instead, after Nelson Mandela was released in 1990, the black majority followed his astonishing example of forgiveness over revenge, and the right-wing paramilitaries were kept in check by the momentum of change being championed by the moderate majority.

Since that momentous election day, South Africa's stock has been on the up amongst the international community. Previously constrained by sanctions, the long-dormant economy was freed of these restrictions. Based on a substantial mining industry, and with a well-developed infrastructure and sophisticated financial and telecommunications system in support, South Africa has grown to become the undisputed economic powerhouse in Africa, and one of the 25 largest economies in the world. On the political front, global and continental leaders accord South Africa

enormous respect, a situation borne out by the role it plays in international and regional organisations and forums. For this, Mandela must take enormous credit. His presidency reversed the process of exclusion by reopening the doors of authority and power that had been so firmly slammed shut because of apartheid. He also played a significant role in building the 'Rainbow Nation' by forging national harmony. Thabo Mbeki, his successor, built on this legacy through his resolute determination to establish Africa and South Africa as a leading power broker in the halls of the United Nations, the Commonwealth and the African Union. A generally positive public sentiment infiltrates all aspects of nationhood, and South Africa has also had much to boast about with regard to its sporting, artistic, cultural, scientific and engineering achievements since 1994.

However, while South Africa enjoys these high approval ratings within the international community, the government has begun to receive far more criticism for its

ABOVE *These high-rise buildings in Sandton, Johannesburg, reflect the rapidly developing status of this commercial centre.*

home record. It has high disapproval ratings on a number of domestic issues. For the majority of the electorate, the honeymoon period is well and truly over, with the euphoria of the Mandela days a dim and distant memory. For them, life today is about struggling with the many challenges South Africa faces, and trying to elect local politicians capable of delivering on their promises. While most of these challenges are to be expected of a young developing nation, some are more menacing, and, if left unchecked, they threaten to undermine the considerable achievements made to date.

Poverty, unemployment and income disparity, the three ugly sisters in economic statistical analysis, are the long-term issues in need of most attention. If the current trends cannot be reversed, then every other concern is of little or no consequence. Despite the strong macroeconomic performance to date, almost 48 per cent of South Africans experience poverty in some form or another, the unemployment rates run somewhere between 26 per cent and

40 per cent (depending on the index used), and South Africa still has one of the highest income and land owner-ship gaps in the world. The government's much-touted solution is the introduction of the Accelerated and Shared Growth Initiative for South Africa (Asgisa), which seeks to halve unemployment and poverty rates by 2014. It aims to achieve this by promoting investment and economic conditions that can deliver sustained growth of more than 6 per cent per annum. This is all well and good on paper, but, to succeed, South Africa needs to contend more vigorously with its global competitors – those developing nations that are attracting more foreign investment than South Africa is. For this to happen, the labour unions, powerful on both the economic and political front, need to be convinced and brought on side. Many have their doubts that this will happen.

The poverty and unemployment statistics feed another major challenge for South Africans: the crime issue. Chilling, and at times even depressing, the unacceptably high levels of crime regularly appear as the number one concern of citizens and foreigners alike. The figures are also a substan-tial hindrance to international investment, and the reason that many skilled and professionally qualified citizens choose to leave South Africa for safer places. This departure is collectively referred to locally as the 'brain drain'; profes-sional skills in fields such as medicine, engineering, public administration, management and a variety of technical and artisan classifications are already in short supply.

The loss of skills exacerbates an additional obstacle to growth – failure in service delivery. It is one thing to be able to collect taxes (something the revenue authorities do remark-ably well), but the benefit of this will eventually be nullified if the funds cannot be efficiently and effectively distributed to a population in need. There have been substantial gains in the provision of housing and electricity, in the laying on of sanitation and drinking water, and in economic empower-ment and the improvement of the social grants system, but the portfolios of police, home affairs, criminal justice and health, for example, have become nothing short of woeful. Investment in education is still way short of requirements, public transport facilities are inadequate, land reform is well behind schedule, the AIDS and HIV statistics remain

unacceptably high, many public hospitals and clinics are in decline, and conservation and sustainability initiatives are mostly ineffective.

Rather disturbingly, the scourge of corruption and crony capitalism is taking hold. Whether as bribery, nepotism or outright theft, these practices are in some way part and parcel of most political processes worldwide, but that's little solace in South Africa when there are obvious signs that the very institutions and people put in place to rid South Africans of them are being undermined. Criminal syndicates are certainly involved, but the suspicion that state-sanctioned subversion may also be an issue is extremely disturbing. With these practices seemingly becoming endemic, and the shameless behaviour of the culprits, could this not be the most critical short-term test this young and still-fragile democracy faces?

But back to the good news. Of course, most of the world knows that South Africa has been appointed as host for the 2010 Football World Cup (www.worldcup2010southafrica. com; www.fifa.com), a first for the continent of Africa. Besides fun and enjoyment, this event is forecast to deliver considerable economic benefits to the nine host cities and the greater

ABOVE *The Titbits Restaurant is a well-known stopover for travellers passing through Springbok in the Northern Cape.*

subcontinent. It is forecast to contribute R21 billion to the GDP, generate R7.2 billion in government taxes, and create more than 135 000 jobs. The 350 000 expected visitors are forecast to spend almost R10 billion.

But why wait until the World Cup to visit South Africa? There is no other country in Africa that offers something for everyone in the way that it does. Incorporating elements of both the developed and less developed worlds, and with a palpable mood that speaks of history in the making, it is an exciting and dynamic place to be. Throw in the cosmopolitan population and cultural diversity, the immense scenic beauty and magnificent outdoors, and the pleasant temperate climate, and there is precious little reason to delay your next vacation. Welcome to South Africa! *Namukelekile eMzantsi Afrika! Le amophetswe mo Afrika Borwa! Welkom in Suid Afrika!*

The following websites offer a wealth of information on South Africa: www.sagoodnews.co.za; www.southafrica.info; www.info.gov.za

15

All that glitters – gold, diamonds and more

If the apartheid era is the one that defines South Africa's political history, then the mining industry is what defines South Africa's economic successes. In fact, it would not be amiss to say that the discovery of diamonds and gold was the most significant event in South Africa's economic, political and social development. The production and export of minerals not only became the foundation for South Africa's industrial expansion, but also brought about the discriminatory political and social conditions that became features of the political landscape: job discrimination, the migrant labour system, the single-sex hostel complexes and the pass laws.

Since the first gems and nuggets were discovered back in the late 1800s, South Africa has been at the forefront of global mining in terms of technology, production and mineral reserves. What until then had been an unremarkable agrarian-based country was, within a few decades, transformed into one of the world's most promising economies. Hustlers and hoods started the rush, but as news spread of further discoveries and the potential reserves that lay beneath the earth, they were joined by miners, financiers and investors who came to claim their slice of the fledgling metal and mineral industries.

DIAMOND DAYS

The first diamond discovery was made in 1866 on a farm in the Hopetown district of the Northern Cape and this was followed by the finding of numerous rich kimberlite pipes around Kimberley in the 1870s, and various alluvial deposits along the Vaal and Orange rivers during the late 1880s. These initial discoveries were followed by those at Cullinan outside Pretoria in 1902, and the finding of alluvial deposits at Kleinzee along the west coast in 1925, the Finsch pipe in the Northern Cape in 1961, and the riches of the Venetia mine along the Limpopo River in the early 1980s.

While South Africa enjoyed early wealth from its diamond deposits, these were soon overtaken in size and richness by larger finds elsewhere – in Russia, Australia, and parts of South America and Africa, most notably. But by then, a company called De Beers had already established itself, and so while South Africa's carat production fell, the global industry in diamonds soon became associated with this giant South African corporation. Now with its primary listing in London, and along with its marketing and sales arm, the Central Selling Organisation, De Beers remains the leading force in the global diamond market.

ABOVE *The vast majority of South Africa's power is generated by coal-fired power stations such as this one outside Vereeniging.*

STRIKING GOLD

Although there were earlier findings of gold in Barberton and Pilgrim's Rest, it is generally accepted that the first major strike of a reef came in 1886 when gold was discovered on a farm immediately south of present-day Johannesburg. Shortly thereafter, and in need of another source for tax revenue, President Paul Kruger officially set off a major rush for gold by declaring numerous farms in the region to be open diggings. The first mining village, later to be known as Johannesburg, was established in December 1886. Word spread across the world, and within a few years there was a major influx of investors, many coming from Europe, and black mine-workers into the Witwatersrand as they came in search of the bounty.

Larger deposits of gold were subsequently found, and today the gold fields of South Africa stretch in an arc, almost 350 km long and over 220 km wide, across Gauteng, North West and into northern Free State. The ore-bearing rocks that make up the Witwatersrand Basin are thought to have collected their gold deposits more than 2.5 billion years ago when rivers washed loads of sediment into an ancient sea that once covered the site. Having produced more than half of the total global tonnage ever mined, the South African gold fields are the richest ever found.

ABOVE *The city of Johannesburg, founded after the discovery of gold in 1886, is well known for the mine dumps that surround parts of the modern city.*

THE RISE OF A MINING INDUSTRY

By 1900, substantial wealth had been generated from gold and diamonds, and the first mining houses had been formed. These mining corporations, controlled by a group of financiers that became known as the 'Randlords', grew to dominate the Johannesburg Securities Exchange. They had the capital and expertise to fund the discovery and expansion of other metal and mineral products – coal, platinum, copper, iron and steel, for example – and to lay the foundations for South Africa's banking and industrial sectors.

Although the South African gold-mining industry is still the world's leading producer, mining analysts have forecast that, at currently known reserves, the industry has passed its heyday. The 1970s were the most productive period, but since then, higher costs of deeper mining and of labour and lower grades of ore have constrained the industry. While South Africa does have a diversified industrial and manufacturing economic base, with major contributions coming from the tourism and financial sectors, the mining sector still remains the ultimate barometer of South Africa's fortunes.

travel
SOUTH AFRICA

PREVIOUS PAGES *Hikers along the Robberg Peninsula in Plettenberg Bay take time out to savour the impressive views.*

ABOVE *The view of a cloud-bedecked Table Mountain from the V&A Waterfront in Cape Town.*

*S*outh Africa has, over the last decade, established itself as one of the leading tourism destinations in the world. During 2006, it received 8.4 million international visitors – second only to Egypt on the continent. Its lodges, hotels and destinations regularly receive top ratings by various recognised international surveys.

In the *Travel & Leisure 2007* World's Best Awards, nine leading South African establishments were listed amongst the world's Top 100 hotels. Singita Sabi Sand was rated the second-best small hotel in the overall category and the best hotel in the Africa and Middle East category. In the same survey, readers for the international magazine rated Cape Town as the tenth-best holiday city in the world, and the best in the Africa and Middle East category. The Cape Grace was voted as having the ninth-best spa in the Africa and Asia-Pacific category.

In the *Condé Nast Traveler* Readers' Choice survey for 2006, South African hotels took seven of the top 15 places in the Top 15 Hotels in Africa category. In the same survey, four establishments were ranked in the global Top 100 Best of the Best category. *Condé Nast* readers also voted Cape Town the number one city in Africa and the eighth best in the world.

ABOVE *The elephants of the Kruger National Park are a feature attraction for wildlife enthusiasts from around the world.*

The hot spots

Measured in terms of visitor numbers, South Africa's top five tourist destinations are the following:

Cape Peninsula – Includes Cape Town, Table Mountain, Cape Point, the V&A Waterfront and the Winelands

Kruger National Park – Includes the private reserves of Sabi Sand and Timbavati

Sun City – A large casino, resort complex and golf course in North West province

Garden Route – A 250-km-long scenic stretch along the southern Cape coast

Northern KwaZulu-Natal – Includes iSimangaliso Wetland Park (formerly Greater St Lucia Wetland Park), the game reserves and historical sites.

World Heritage Sites

The United Nations Educational, Scientific and Cultural Organisation (UNESCO), through the international treaty known as the Convention Concerning the Protection of the World Cultural and Natural Heritage (http://whc.unesco.org), seeks to 'encourage the identification, protection and preservation of cultural and natural heritage around the world considered to be of outstanding value to humanity'. Globally there are presently 851 World Heritage Sites listed in 141 countries. Africa has 77 sites and South Africa eight.

BELOW *With the Tsitsikamma mountains as a backdrop, Plettenberg Bay along the southern Cape coast has some of the country's finest beaches.*

ISIMANGALISO WETLAND PARK

Formerly known as the Greater St Lucia Wetland Park, this system was proclaimed in 1999. This natural site is the largest estuarine system in Africa. Comprising various ecosystems, it covers 234 566 ha along the northern KwaZulu-Natal coast and boasts an immense biodiversity that includes more than 500 bird species.

ROBBEN ISLAND

This small island, lying 11 km off Cape Town, was proclaimed a cultural site in 1999. Once a leper colony back in the late 1800s, and then a military post before and after the Second World War, it became known worldwide after the apartheid government turned it into a maximum-security prison for political prisoners. It was here that Nelson Mandela, its most famous inmate, spent most of his 27 years behind bars.

FOSSIL HOMINID SITES OF STERKFONTEIN, SWARTKRANS, KROMDRAAI AND ENVIRONS

Known as 'The Cradle of Humankind', and proclaimed in 1999, this 47 000 ha cultural site just north of Johannesburg contains one of the world's richest concentrations of human and other fossils. The cave and valley

ABOVE *A vast coastline comprises the primary feature of the iSimangaliso Wetland Park, one of South Africa's eight World Heritage Sites.*

complex of Sterkfontein, Swartkrans and Kromdraai has produced almost 1 000 hominid specimens, some dating back as far as 3.5 million years.

UKHAHLAMBA-DRAKENSBERG PARK

Proclaimed in 2000, this mixed cultural and natural site is recognised for its outstanding natural beauty as well as the immense collection of rock art paintings found throughout what is the highest mountain range in southern Africa. The site covers 243 000 ha along the KwaZulu-Natal–Lesotho border.

MAPUNGUBWE CULTURAL LANDSCAPE

The Iron Age site of Mapungubwe, in far northern South Africa, along the border with Zimbabwe and Botswana, was proclaimed in 2003 for its historical and cultural value. Unearthed only in the early 1900s, it was the base for a kingdom that lasted 400 years before being abandoned in the fourteenth century.

CAPE FLORAL REGION PROTECTED AREAS

This natural site of the Cape Floral Kingdom was proclaimed in 2004 for its extremely rich plant diversity. While covering only 0.04 per cent of the world's land area, the region contains 3 per cent of all plant species, of which 31.9 per cent are endemic. It contains eight protected areas along the southern tip of South Africa, including Table Mountain, Kirstenbosch National Botanical Garden and the Cederberg mountain range.

VREDEFORT DOME

A natural site proclaimed in 2005, the Vredefort Dome consists of a crater formed by a massive meteorite strike thought to have occurred almost two billion years ago. The

ABOVE *Robben Island, proclaimed a World Heritage Site in 1999, lies 11 km off Cape Town. It was here that Nelson Mandela spent most of his 27 years behind bars.*

site, near the town of Vredefort in the Free State, measures approximately 10 km in diameter.

RICHTERSVELD CULTURAL AND BOTANICAL LANDSCAPE

Proclaimed in 2007, this site covers 160 000 ha of mountain desert scenery in the far northwest of the country. Three Nama communities, many of whose people still practise a semi-nomadic pastoral lifestyle, live in the greater region.

Tourism offices and websites

The following websites are well worth exploring when planning a trip to South Africa:

General tourism information – www.southafrica.info; www.satourism.co.za; www.indaba-southafrica.co.za; www.southafrica.net; www.southafricaexplore.co.za; www.routes.co.za

General accommodation – www.wheretostay.co.za; www.sa-venues.com; www.portfoliocollection.com; www.i-escapes.com; www.aatravel.co.za

Bed and breakfast accommodation – www.bedandbreakfast.co.za

Backpacking accommodation – www.backpack.co.za; www.drivesouthafrica.co.za

Alternative routes – www.alternativeroute.net

South African national parks – www.parks-sa.co.za

South Africa is well represented at a provincial level, with each province having its own tourism office and website:

Eastern Cape Tourism Board – www.ectourism.co.za

Free State Tourism Board – www.dteea.fs.gov.za

Gauteng Tourism Authority – www.gauteng.net

KwaZulu-Natal Tourism Authority – www.kzn.org.za

Limpopo Tourism Board – www.golimpopo.com

North West Province Parks and Tourism Board – www.tourismnorthwest.co.za

Mpumalanga Tourism Authority – www.mpumalanga.com

Northern Cape Tourism Authority – www.northerncape.org.za

Western Cape Tourism Board – www.tourismcapetown.co.za

Outside the major urban areas, most small towns have a tourism office linked to a website of some sort, but it is important to note that these sites may carry only those establishments and services contributing to the running costs of the tourism office and website.

Since 1994, numerous South African towns, airports and roads and various geographical features have undergone name changes. Somewhat controversial because of the political nature of the process, the changes are nevertheless an attempt to redress the naming that occurred under apartheid governments and to correct misspellings common during the colonial era. Maps, texts and guide and travel books published before 2004 may still have many of the old names. For updated information on names go to the following website: www.mapstudio.co.za

ABOVE *The Cape Floral Kingdom covers a number of reserves and mountain ranges across the southern and southwestern Cape. These hikers are traversing the mountain section of the Whale Trail in the De Hoop Nature Reserve.*

Planning your trip

Planning a trip to South Africa can be a daunting exercise. It is a large country and, besides the wildlife and outdoor options for which Africa is traditionally known, there are a host of other reasons to visit. This makes the choice of destinations, activities and accommodation almost limitless.

In order to make it easier, this book covers only what we believe to be the better regions and destinations in South Africa. And while we do not focus on accommodation options, we have listed specific establishments that we believe are worthwhile. The websites and ideas listed will ensure that you are able to plan your trip successfully. For wildlife options, see the On Safari chapter, and if you are interested in travelling the countryside, see Country Roads. Listed below are some other fantastic reasons why you should visit South Africa.

ADVENTURE ADDICTS

Adventure tourism has, in recent years, taken the world by storm. An entire culture based on the needs of the adrenaline junkie has emerged, and it involves the gear, the activities and the environment. The choice of activities is vast: South Africa's excellent climate, diverse landscape, good infra-structure and relatively small local population participating in these pursuits provide a fabulously uncrowded playground. And the country is well geared to this provision, with numerous highly respected operators and outfitters. For the purposes of this book, only a select few are detailed.

When choosing an activity and operator, please consider the impact you may have on the environment: tyres, boots and well-worn routes cause erosion, the use of dune and beach may disturb birds' nests, and discarded gear and litter don't easily biodegrade in South Africa's climate.

For a comprehensive list of activities and further useful information go to: www.sa-venues.com/activities; www.activeafrica.co.za; www.wildthing.co.za

Hiking

There are a number of South African multi-day hikes that have become local institutions to the outdoor fraternity. They certainly rate as some of the best hiking experiences in the world. Be advised: book well in advance. The most well known of these is the Otter Trail along the Tsitsikamma coast on the Garden Route. This five-day trail hugs the undulating shoreline, passing through dense indigenous coastal and montane forest and fynbos. The frequent river crossings add to the adventure (www.mtoecotourism.co.za; e-mail: info@mtoecotourism.co.za or ecotour@safcol.co.za).

The Whale Trail, along the coast of the De Hoop Nature Reserve (see the On Safari chapter) rivals the Otter Trail in being rated South Africa's premier coastal hike (www.capenature.org.za). Other great coastal hikes include the Oystercatcher Trail, starting in Mossel Bay, and the Dolphin Trail, a less demanding Tsitsikamma experience (www.oystercatchertrail.co.za).

The Eastern Cape's Wild Coast also hosts a number of wonderful sun-and-sea trails. These are well organised experiences, and each night is spent in a different, delightful beach hotel along the coast (www.wildcoastwalk.co.za; www.wildcoast.co.za).

South Africa's first ever mega-hike is a product of an exciting conservation project known as the Eden to Addo Corridor Initiative. A fairly new endeavour, this hike has the makings of a grand journey on foot. It could become a legendary African experience (e-mail: hike@edentoaddo.co.za).

The highest mountain range in southern Africa, the magnificent uKhahlamba/Drakensberg range in KwaZulu-Natal, offers a multitude of trails, with something for everyone. These mountains provide it all, from scenic day walks to demanding hikes for the experienced mountaineer (see the Country Roads chapter) to challenging rock-climbing routes for the adventurous.

Table Mountain, the heart of the city of Cape Town, is a hiker's mecca. Being able to access such rugged beauty just minutes from the city centre makes this an extraordinary destination. Up until recently, the mountain offered only day trails but now there are multi-day options which allow you to traverse the plateau of this dramatic geological asset (www.hoerikwaggotrails.co.za). Tackling Lion's Head during a full moon period is a particularly spectacular walk.

Red Stone Hills is an immensely scenic area outside Calitzdorp in the Klein Karoo.

Rock climbing

South Africa has an abundance of rugged rock and soaring cliffs, providing perfect pitches for all levels of climber. Table Mountain, once again, reveals its magnificence as a playground on Cape Town's doorstep. Its sandstone and Cape granite rock faces provide excellent opportunities for traditional and sport climbing.

Two to three hours north of Cape Town are the Cederberg mountains. These offer world-class bouldering and boast some of South Africa's best traditional rock-climbing routes.

The uKhahlamba/Drakensberg range in KwaZulu-Natal is an obvious place to head to for an endless selection of traditional climbing, including some exciting ice climbs during the winter. The eastern Free State, near Harrismith, along the northern foothills of the uKhahlamba/Drakensberg range, offers a series of good bolted climbs known as Mt Everest.

Mpumalanga boasts world-renowned climbing in Waterval Boven. Here you will find more than 500 routes and a whole lot more unclimbed rock face awaiting you. For climbers based in the north of the country, Blouberg in Limpopo and the Magaliesberg in North West are great climbing hot spots for the hard-core climber as well as the novice.

The Mountain Club of South Africa (www.mcsa.org. za), founded in 1891, is affiliated to the International Mountaineering and Climbing Federation (UIAA). It offers climbing, mountaineering and hiking opportunities to all members, access to routes, competition climbing and mountain search and rescue. It is also involved with a number of mountain-based conservation programmes.

The Cape Town School of Mountaineering offers training, guided trips and customised climbing coaching (www.ctsm. co.za). For reliable information on route-grading systems in South Africa, go to www.peakhigh.co.za. For comprehensive guides to the country's climbing world, try www.saclimb. co.za and www.climb.co.za. Get climbing gear from RockSport Mountain and Outdoor (www.rocksport.co.za). City Rock Indoor Climbing, in Cape Town, is the largest climbing gym in South Africa (www.cityrock.co.za). The leading local climbing magazine is *SA Mountain* (www.samountainmag.com).

OPPOSITE *Durban is the surf capital of South Africa. The warm Indian Ocean allows for year-round access to the water.*

Bungee jumping

South Africa has the dubious honour of hosting the world's highest bungee jump, at 216 m. The Bloukrans Bridge along the Garden Route sees hundreds of thrill seekers hurl themselves into thin air (Tel: +27 42 281-1458).

Head west along the same route on the N2 towards Cape Town and you'll come across the decommissioned Gouritz Bridge, which offers a mere 65 m fall. Tandem jumps and bridge swings are other slightly less fearsome options available here (Tel: +27 44 697-7001; www.faceadrenalin.com).

Surfing

The South African surf scene, made famous by *The Endless Summer* movies, proffers world-class waves. Both Durban and Cape Town offer surf just minutes from the suburbs. The Indian Ocean, which provides Durban with its rolling breakers, is warm all year round; no wetsuits are needed. Head down to New Pier; there are so many breaks here that the locals don't have to defend their turf (www.surfconditions.co.za).

In contrast, Cape Town's Atlantic Ocean is cold. Don the suit, hood and booties and head to where it's happening: Clifton, Llandudno, Camps Bay, and even Sea Point, Long Beach or Kommetjie (www.garysurf.com; www.sunscene. co.za). Muizenberg, on the warmer False Bay, has safe, easy surf, perfect for the novice (www.roxysurfschool.co.za).

Travelling north from Cape Town will take you to Elands Bay, which featured in the movie *The Endless Summer II*. It's cold, but when it works it's world class (www.elandsbay.net).

Going along the Garden Route will get you to Victoria Bay (known to surfers as Vic Bay). Hopefully you'll find it working on a quiet weekday in winter when you may even have it all to yourself. Plettenberg Bay's surf is inconsistent, but this bay is so beautiful that it's worth a try (www. jaminadventures.com; e-mail: info@jaminadventures.com). Cape St Francis and Jeffreys Bay (J-Bay) are world famous. J-Bay's Supertubes is South Africa's most consistent wave and surfers flock from all over the globe to experience this legendary right break (www.jaybay.co.za).

The Eastern Cape's Wild Coast is spectacular and has some excellent surf, but it is a treacherous coastline with a reputation for shark-infested river mouths. This may be urban legend but nevertheless chat to the locals at Coffee

Bay and Port St Johns before heading for the water. Mdumbe, Ntlonyane (Breezy Point) and Mbhashe River are just some of the most rewarding breaks in the area.

Paragliding

Head to Cape Town, where Table Mountain offers great flying. Get a bird's-eye view of the city before dropping down beside the beautiful Camps Bay beach.

The Garden Route provides the country's safest and most varied coastal flying. Ridge-soar over beaches, lagoons and saltwater lakes. The best flying is in January, when the onshore winds are steady but not too strong (www. paraglidingsa.com).

Great inland flying happens in the Western Cape near Porterville, and of course, the uKhahlamba/Drakensberg range in KwaZulu-Natal provides a magnificent aerial playground (Tel. SAHPA: +27 12 668-1219; www. sahpa.co.za; www.paraglide-south-africa.com).

Kite surfing

Kite surfing is a relatively new sport in South Africa but imported technology, coupled with consistent winds, safe shores and fantastic seas, has enabled South Africa to become a leading destination for enthusiasts. Cape Town is the kite-surfing capital with a first-class kiting school situated in Bloubergstrand (www.cabrinha.co.za). Muizenberg beach, with its wide, safe surf and regular onshore wind, is another perfect playground.

Up the windswept West Coast, situated on a large lagoon, is Langebaan. Long recognised as a superlative board-sailing destination, it is now being dominated by the kites. Accommodation owners are well accustomed to providing drying racks for gear.

In the Eastern Cape, Port Elizabeth is aptly nicknamed the Windy City. In normal circumstances this is not usually a feature attraction, but for a kite surfer, it's heaven (www. windswept.co.za).

Mountain biking

A great climate allows for good off-road bike riding across South Africa. Mountain biking is well established and well supported and will satisfy any level of rider.

In the north, the Magaliesberg Protected Natural Environment has some great technical, as well as some easy, riding (www.mtbsa.co.za; www.mtbroutes.co.za).

Cape Town's single-track rides in the forest on the slopes of Table Mountain are great fun. Head for the arboretum in Tokai. Experienced riders can do the uphill slog at sunset, don the head torch at dusk and wind their way through the trees by torchlight.

The Garden Route has arguably the best variety of trails in South Africa, with the Harkerville Forest Trails, between Plettenberg Bay and Knysna, being the most popular. There are four different options of trail, graded from easy to difficult and well marked with different colour indicators (The Bike Shop, Plettenberg Bay, Tel: +27 44 533-1111; e-mail: plettcycles@mweb.co.za).

Sea kayaking

There is very little protected water off the South African coast, making sea kayaking that much more exciting. There are endless opportunities for the experienced paddler, but for the inexperienced guided trips are advisable.

Cape Town's False Bay provides an opportunity to paddle close to the shore and see the penguin colony at Simon's Town from a new vantage point (www.kayak.co.za; www. seakayak.co.za). North from Cape Town, on the West Coast, nothing could beat a trip across the kelp beds in a slow boat on a balmy day (www.ratrace.co.za).

Plettenberg Bay's relatively protected waters provide unbeatable paddles with dolphins, and during the winter months kayaking is a great way to watch whales (www. oceanadventures.co.za).

iSimangaliso Wetland Park's eastern shores offer gentle paddles in the wilderness and a great way to watch birds — but steer clear of hippos! (Tel: +27 35 550-5036; e-mail: dandy@telkomsa.net).

White-water rafting and kayaking

The best-known river in South Africa, the Orange River, provides the most popular commercial white-water rafting. Bordering Namibia, this river meanders through spectacular desert and mountainous terrain. There are a number of adrenaline sections, but almost all the trip options include long stretches of gentle drifting through magnificent scenery, interspersed with some fantastic fun (www.felixunite.com; www.orangeriverrafting.com).

The Western Cape is home to creek kayaking – narrow, steep and technical. The white water is largely dependent on the winter rainfall. Both the Palmiet and Doring rivers provide some testy technical rafting and kayaking. They also run through wonderful countryside (www.aquatrails.co.za; www.gravity.co.za).

KwaZulu-Natal is where the heart of South African river culture lies. The Mkomazi River has a fabulous 12–24 km run of grade-three white water. Other options are the Mgeni, which makes up a part of the famous Dusi Canoe Marathon, and the Buffalo River in northern Zululand. This is highly rated as a rafting destination. Adding to the thrill are the potential sightings of wildlife, as this river winds through a number of private game reserves (www.canoesa.org.za).

WINING AND DINING

For wine lovers, South Africa's Western Cape is worth a visit for the wine industry alone. Not only does the region produce world-class wines at very competitive prices, but its wine-producing areas have to be some of the most stunning in the world (see the City to City chapter).

During the years of apartheid-induced isolation, the South African wine industry hit a slump and became dominated by a handful of historic estates and co-operatives. Without the benefits of knowledge exchange with other countries and the required financial upkeep, many wines became uninspiring at best, and at worst, unpalatable. Today's story is a far happier one. The industry has grown substantially, and there is an enormous amount of constructive competition, both locally and from abroad. Exciting new boutique wineries spring up with every new vintage. South African wines increasingly win international awards and the culture of wine drinking expands every year.

Hand in hand with this thrilling development, of course, comes food! Many of the wine estates have fabulous restaurants where the idea is to couple good food with great wines. International exposure has resulted in the emergence of a creative cuisine, which fuses traditional and local foods with global dishes.

ABOVE *Mountain bikers will find South Africa a fantastic destination as there are a large number of trails spread across the country.*

South Africa boasts many excellent restaurants. The country hotels, lodges and safari camps have developed a reputation for serving award-winning meals. If you are a true foodie, travel the country following great chefs who either own or are employed at these establishments (www.goodcooks.co.za).

The premier South African wine magazine, *Wine*, is an excellent source of information and wine ratings. The International Annual Wine Guide 2007 was recently awarded to *Platter's South African Wines* (www.platteronline.com).

SPORTS ENTHUSIASTS

No matter whether you are a fanatical supporter or a keen participant, South Africa offers a host of exciting world-class sporting events.

Fans and supporters

Fans and supporters annually have a choice of international soccer, cricket and rugby matches that are played at various venues in the major cities, and several internationally recognised golf, athletics and boxing tournaments are also held every year. For the most recently updated calendar covering all sporting events, go to www.supersport.co.za

ABOVE *The Camps Bay beachfront in Cape Town is a favoured destination for those seeking good restaurants and a lively bar and club scene.*

The following websites offer useful information: South African Rugby (www.sarfu.org.za), South African Cricket (www.cricket.co.za) and South African Golf (www.saga.co.za). Supporters wanting to book packages while following their home nation on tour should consult SuperSport Travel (www.puresport.co.za).

Participants

South Africa has a multitude of superb golf courses throughout the country. Amateur golfers wanting to tour South Africa while playing golf can contact South African Golf Tour (www.sagolftour.co.za).

For participants who enjoy exciting and challenging events, South Africa offers several that are recognised the world over as being amongst the leading contests in their codes. Because they are all extremely popular, participants should submit their entry forms early.

The Comrades Marathon – Run annually in June between Durban and Pietermaritzburg, this 90 km ultramarathon is one of the most punishing on the annual calendar (www. comrades.com).

The Two Oceans Marathon – Another highly regarded ultramarathon, the Two Oceans takes runners along an extremely scenic 56 km course around the Cape Peninsula, including Chapman's Peak Drive and Hout Bay (www. twooceansmarathon.org.za).

The *Cape Argus*/Pick n Pay Cycle Tour – Covering the most scenic roads of the Cape Peninsula, this very popular 105.6 km cycle tour takes place in March every year. It has more than 25 000 entrants (www.cycletour.co.za).

The Cape Epic – This 900 km ride is regarded as one of the world's most gruelling mountain-biking events. Starting in Knysna, the cyclists cover some of the most testing mountain ranges, before ending outside Cape Town eight days later (www.cape-epic.com).

The Dusi Canoe Marathon – Although labelled as a canoe marathon, this three-day event often entails as much running as paddling. It takes place at the beginning of the year and is run on the Mgeni and Msunduzi rivers in KwaZulu-Natal (www.dusi.org.za).

BIRDING

South Africa is a fantastic destination for keen birders: the species list is more than 850 birds, including 58 endemics, and there is an impressive diversity of habitat ranging from subtropical forests to arid semideserts. The local birding community is extremely active, with numerous bird clubs spread throughout the country, and there are a large number of top guides available in all the main birding areas. For a comprehensive list of the clubs, their meeting schedules and recognised birding routes throughout South Africa, contact BirdLife South Africa (www.birdlife.org.za; www.birdingroutes.co.za).

Birding hot spots include the Cape Floral Kingdom in the Western Cape, the central regions of the uKhahlamba/Drakensberg mountain range, Wakkerstroom, northern KwaZulu-Natal, the Pafuri region of the Kruger National Park, Nylsvlei and the arid regions of the Northern Cape. Other interesting websites are: www.sabirding.co.za; www. africageographic.com; www.birdingafrica.com

While the coast of the southern Cape offers the most rewarding pelagic birding, trips are also possible from Port

ABOVE *The Water Thick-knee is commonly seen along water courses and in wetland areas.*
LEFT *White-fronted Bee-eaters are typically found along the banks of large river systems and on the fringes of freshwater expanses in the north of the country.*

LUCKY NGWENYA

Based in the small country town of Wakkerstroom in Mpumalanga, Lucky is one of the region's resident guides for BirdLife South Africa. After completing his schooling, he joined BirdLife in 2000 and helped build the four hides located just outside the town.

Working amidst birds inspired him to enrol in various courses covering guide training and birds, and in 2003 he took his first guests into the field. Lucky is familiar with all the habitats in the region, but particularly likes forest and grassland birding.

To make use of his guiding services, contact him at: Tel: +27 72 483-6668 or c/o e-mail: wetlandscountryhouse@telkomsa.net

Elizabeth, East London, Richards Bay and Durban. Day trips on board a motorised boat are the best way to view the seabirds, and the winter months from May to August are the most rewarding.

RECOGNISED ROUTES

For ease of marketing, a number of recognised tourism routes are listed in South Africa. These cover everything from birding and wildlife routes to wine and whaling options. Many will be covered in some way in the following chapters, but here are some of the best:

Garden Route – From Mossel Bay to St Francis Bay (www.gardenroute.org.za)

Winelands Route – The original wine route outside Cape Town (www.wineroute.co.za)

Route 62 – Classic regional route through the Little Karoo (www.route62.co.za)

North Coast – Coastal towns immediately north of Durban (www.dolphincoast.kzn.org.za)

South Coast – Coastal towns to the south of Durban (www.southcoast.kzn.org.za)

Sunshine Coast – From St Francis Bay to East London (www.suncoast.co.za)

Whale Route – The coast between Cape Town and Hermanus (www.whaleroute.com)

Elephant Coast – Coast and wilderness areas of northern KwaZulu-Natal (www.elephantcoast.kzn.org.za)

Battlefields Route – The Zulu, Brit and Boer battlefields of KwaZulu-Natal (www.battlefields.kzn.org.za)

Raptor Route – Raptor viewing in the Northern Cape (www.places.co.za)

Highlands Meander – South Africa's premier fly-fishing spots in Mpumalanga (www.dullstroom.co.za)

Magalies Meander – The Magaliesberg mountain range (www.magaliesmeander.co.za)

Midlands Meander – The KwaZulu-Natal Midlands (www.kzn.org.za)

Roaring Kalahari Route – The Kalahari region (www.roaringkalahari.co.za)

Southernmost Region of Africa Route – A circular route that takes in the southern Cape and the southernmost tip of Africa (www.viewoverberg.com).

The gay and lesbian scene

South Africa's Constitution is one of the most progressive in the world, and it includes legal protection for gay and lesbian rights. Because of this, gay and lesbian travellers generally find South Africa a far more welcoming country than it was before the transition to democracy in 1994. Having said this, it is also the case that in some areas old prejudices die hard. This is particularly so in the mostly conservative country towns of the central and northern regions of South Africa. Travellers to these regions may find their options limited.

While all the major urban areas have a variety of accommodation, clubs and bars, Johannesburg and Cape Town have the most active and open gay scenes. Occurring annually in December, the Mother City Queer Project (www.mcqp.co.za) has become a calendar highlight in Cape Town, not only for the gay community, but also for many city residents who enjoy the fun and pizzazz of stylish costume parties.

The following websites will be of help when planning a trip to South Africa: www.gaysouthafrica.org.za; www.exit.co.za; www.wanderwomen.co.za; www.gaypleasure.com; www.outinafrica.co.za

Travel with care and caution

You are about to embark on a journey to one of the world's leading nature-based destinations. While your daily experiences will mostly be fun-filled and immensely rewarding, it is nonetheless important to be aware of some environmental and conservation issues that affect everybody in South Africa. All the destinations and regions you are about to visit – whether an urban metropolis, a rural landscape or a national park or private reserve – will be affected in some way.

It is also important to bear in mind that while sensitive and responsible tourism generally has plenty of advantages, it also has negative aspects that impact on the environment and local communities. Presently, there is no universally accepted understanding or definition of – or measurement tool for – the notion of an ecologically aware operator or traveller. What is loosely termed 'ecotourism' or 'nature-based tourism' is still very much a work in progress. In general, the aim is to travel lightly and respectfully, leaving as little impact as possible, while contributing in a meaningful way to the host country and its people. The awareness and responsibility you display while in South Africa and the message you take home with you can make a significant difference.

TIPS FOR SENSITIVE AND RESPONSIBLE TOURISM

- Flying in jet aircraft contributes to carbon emissions and global warming, and while only contributing approximately 5 per cent at the moment, this is forecast to grow to almost 15 per cent over the next 25 years. Thoughtful planning, which minimises the number of flights and the flight time, will help, as will using trains or public-transport systems, where possible, once you are in South Africa, and including cycling and walking options in your trip.

- If the planning and booking of your trip is being done by an agent or operator, seek out one that is highly regarded for embracing the principles of sensitive and respectful travel.

- If you are doing a self-drive or self-planned trip, try to include operations, lodges and homes that reflect South African society and those that embrace sound conservation and environmental principles. Wherever possible, try to buy local produce rather than imported goods.

- Inform your agent, operator or local tourism authority of incidents, events or practices that are offensive, insensitive or in contravention of generally accepted environmental laws and practices. You are within your rights to ask the operator you are with or the camp or lodge at which you are staying about their environmental attitudes and practices.

- A variety of animal species are killed to provide crafts, curios and trinkets of a souvenir nature. Consider this fact before buying any product made from wildlife. Commonly sold items include ivory; elephant-hair bangles; shark- and lion-tooth pendants; porcupine-quill frames and lamp shades; and bags, belts, rugs and furniture items made from the skins of a variety of wild species.

- Wood carvings, found in all markets and curio shops throughout South Africa, are a favourite souvenir for visitors. These are most often made from hardwood trees, many of which are threatened or endangered species. Ask your guide for advice before buying any carvings.
- Scuba divers and beach goers to coastal destinations will be offered a variety of sea shells and turtle and coral products through curio stalls and beach vendors. If you purchase them, you will be contributing to the destruction of the reef systems as well as the depletion of the species involved. (In most cases, the export of these products is illegal.)
- The pressure placed on wild animals at sightings in many parks and reserves is one of the most unsavoury aspects of the tourism industry. Be respectful of the critical distance for each animal species. It is not acceptable to provoke wildlife into uncharacteristic behaviour.
- Trophy hunting is practised in various forms in South Africa. This includes the horrific practice of shooting animals in cages or small, confined areas. Operators offering this 'canned hunting' are often also involved in programmes for the breeding of wild animals. Please inform your agent or the local tourism authority if you encounter these practices.
- If you hire your own 4x4 vehicle, stick to recognised trails and routes and avoid driving on any sensitive terrain such as gravel plains and wetlands. The damage caused may take decades to recover. Driving on any beach or across coastal dunes is not allowed.
- Many towns, camps and lodges are situated in regions that experience scarce or erratic water supplies. The water-saving measures employed are necessary and are in place to ensure the sustainability of the community or operation.
- Respect the local people and their cultures, particularly those who are living a more traditional life. Consider that your presence may be an intrusion, and do not buy

ABOVE *O.R. Tambo International in Johannesburg is Africa's largest and busiest airport.*
OPPOSITE *South Africa offers visitors a wide variety of cultural experiences, including the Ndebele cultural village at Botshabelo in Mpumalanga.*

obviously valuable family or community artefacts or use Western goods to barter.

- Being supportive of local conservation, community and educational projects is generally of greater benefit than you may think. Your contribution may make the difference between success and failure.
- Be aware of 'greenwashing', which is the practice of deceiving unwary people, either through labelling or direct marketing, into believing that a particular operator or product adheres to the principles of environmental awareness when perhaps it does not.
- To find out more about responsible tourism and fair trade in tourism, visit the websites of Fair Trade Tourism (www.tourismconcern.org), Fair Trade in Tourism South Africa (www.fairtourismsa.org.za) and the South African Department of Environmental Affairs and Tourism (www.environment.gov.za).

PREVIOUS PAGES *The Orange River meanders its way through the /Ai-/Ais/Richtersveld Transfrontier Park.*

ABOVE *Klaarstroom, a typical Karoo village, lies at the foot of the Swartberg mountains.*

*A*frica's southernmost country is generally regarded as the colossus of the continent and, as the marketing slogan goes, 'a world in one country'. It's the economic powerhouse of Africa, carries the most political clout and influence on the continent and, after Egypt, attracts the highest number of annual visitors.

Blessed with an array of spectacular natural and cultural assets, and linked by a well-developed transport and tourism infrastructure, South Africa offers a selection of exciting possibilities combining wilderness, coastal and city attractions, all within comfortable distances of each other. And weather-wise, other than the southern Cape, which experiences cold and wet winters mid-year, you can readily travel in most parts of the country throughout the year.

Top attractions

THE KAROO

The vast semi-arid and sparsely populated hinterlands of both the Little Karoo and the Great Karoo are South Africa's greatest and most unique attraction. While the sweeping vistas, often desolate and bleak, and the scenic mountain passes, steep and rugged, are so appealing, it's the quirky quaintness and honest charm of life in the country towns that so enriches time spent here. And no matter where you are, solitude and tranquillity are constant companions.

COUNTRY ROADS

If the heartbeat of a country is to be felt in the pulse of its cities, then the character will surely be found amidst the small towns and villages of the countryside. Pack your car, pick up a rental or simply hop on a bus and travel the back roads and dust roads to experience the essence and diversity of traditional South African life.

BELOW *A bird's-eye view of Cape Town from Table Mountain.*

Winter snows blanket the uKhahlamba/Drakensberg mountains in the New England region of the Eastern Cape.

Sunrise over the Coffee Bay region of the Wild Coast.

ABOVE *A journey of giraffes seen in the early-morning light.*

CAPE TOWN

For global travellers, South Africa's oldest and most popular city has become one of the world's truly great hang-outs. While the lure is an appealing mix of natural, night-time and nautical pleasures, it's the comfort of the mountain, the easy-going nature of the multicultural citizenry and the outdoor lifestyle that really makes one feel at home.

THE WILD COAST

Somewhat remote, and distinctly rural and subtropical, this coastal paradise is famed for its rustic and laid-back vacations at the seaside. While it's always a heap of fun in the sun and surf, mixing with the Xhosa locals provides for a fascinating cross-cultural experience, and don't come away without having tackled one of the amazing coastal hikes. The region abounds with charming family hotels and lodges, and for those on budgets, there are some celebrated backpacker stop-offs along the way.

PLETTENBERG BAY AND ROBBERG

In the centre of the celebrated Garden Route, the coastal town of Plettenberg Bay, with its Robberg Peninsula, is undoubt-edly the highlight. Spread along the shores and rolling hills of this sweeping bay, the town offers spectacular views from almost every point. With its endless white beaches and safe swimming, this old whaling station and fishing village has, in recent years, boomed to become one of South Africa's most popular seaside destinations. Avoid the December crowds and you'll be rewarded with the perfect beach holiday.

SPRING FLOWERS

During the spring months, the greater Namaqualand region in the Northern Cape becomes a stunning blaze of colour as carpets of flowers emerge with the onset of warmer temperatures. More than 4 000 species of wild flowers and succulents lie dormant in these semidesert soils, awaiting the winter rainfall. In the following spring's sunshine, they burst forth in a magnificent display that may, in places, range as far as the eye can see.

KRUGER NATIONAL PARK

Massive in size, extraordinarily diverse and packed with plant and animal life, Kruger has a world-renowned reputation for offering a wildlife experience that ranks amongst the most accessible and rewarding in Africa. In fact, for many South Africans, the greater park has become something of an institution and is viewed as the country's most treasured natural asset. From walking trails, campsites and self-catering bungalows to some of the world's finest safari lodges in the private reserves of Sabi Sand and Timbavati, Kruger offers something for everyone.

RICHTERSVELD CULTURAL AND BOTANICAL LANDSCAPE

Rugged, harsh and dramatic, this spectacular mountain desert is South Africa's most recent World Heritage Site. It's also the country's great escape, as it is well off any of the recognised routes for tourists. Time out in these remote and scenic landscapes – outside the recognised holiday periods – is likely to be time spent totally alone.

UKHAHLAMBA/DRAKENSBERG MOUNTAIN RANGE

This massive mountain range dominates what is known as the Great Escarpment. The stretch that straddles parts of KwaZulu-Natal, Free State and Eastern Cape is certainly the most impressive. Magnificently imposing in places, the mountains and their peaks offer an outstanding variety of hiking trails and the most testing of climbing options. Those simply in search of scenery head to the southern sections around Barkly East and Rhodes, or to the Royal Natal National Park.

KGALAGADI TRANSFRONTIER PARK

The scrub-covered, orange-and-red landscapes of the arid Kgalagadi, Africa's first transfrontier conservation area, offer another option for those in search of remoteness. While the dry winter months offer the best game-viewing, the summer rains bring this otherwise parched region of the Kalahari to glorious life and herald the arrival of all the migratory bird species. Although somewhat more accessible than the IAi-IAis/Richtersveld Transfrontier Park, there is a vastness to the Kgalagadi Transfrontier Park that allows a powerful sense of seclusion.

ABOVE *Table Mountain and the upper cable station provide a dramatic backdrop to a mosque in Cape Town's city centre.*

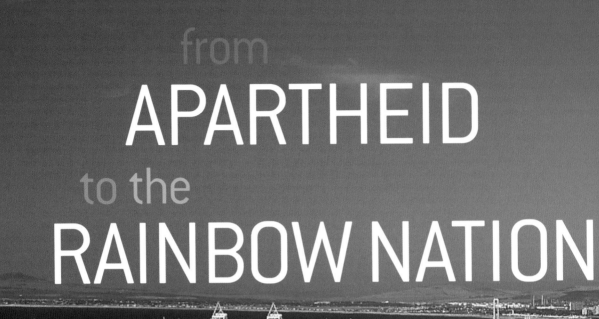

from
APARTHEID
to the
RAINBOW NATION

PREVIOUS PAGES *This prominent mural is along De Waal Drive, a major freeway leading into the city of Cape Town.*

ABOVE *Low-cost housing projects are a common sight on the outskirts of most cities and towns.*

*T*he making of South Africa has been a turbulent process filled with conquest, violent conflicts and political up-
heavals. Because of this, the interpretation and writing of South Africa's history has often been controversial.
While the turmoil amongst the Nguni groups during the early 1800s and the divisions within the black anti-apartheid groups
still attract differing accounts, many academics and teachers of the apartheid era (between 1948 and 1990) were guilty of
gross fabrication and the misrepresentation of events. This resulted in an extremely one-sided narrative put forward by racist
historians and politicians. With the dawn of democracy in the early 1990s, the Rainbow Nation – a term first coined by then
Archbishop Desmond Tutu – was born. This set the course of reconciliation that has allowed the distortions to be corrected.

At a glance

THE GOVERNMENT AND THE JUDICIAL SYSTEM

- The Republic of South Africa is a constitutional and
  multiparty democracy with an independent reserve bank
  and judiciary, and a free press. The Constitution, which
  contains a Bill of Rights, is the supreme law in South Africa.
- South Africa consists of nine provinces: Eastern Cape, Free
  State, Gauteng, KwaZulu-Natal, Limpopo, Mpumalanga,
  Northern Cape, North West and Western Cape.
- Government is carried out by three interconnected arms:
  executive, legislative and judicial. It is administered at
  three levels: national, provincial and local. At the national
  and provincial levels there are various advisory bodies
  drawn from traditional leaders.
- South Africa has a parliamentary system with two
  chambers. The National Assembly has 400 members, who
  are elected by popular vote under a system of proportional
  representation to serve five-year terms. The second
  chamber is the National Council of Provinces, which has
  90 members (10 from each of the nine provinces), who
  serve five-year terms.
- The President is both Head of State and Head of
  Government. The President, Deputy President, Speaker of
  the National Assembly and appointed Cabinet Ministers
  form the executive branch of the government.
- Pretoria is the administrative capital and the de facto
  official capital city. Cape Town is the legislative capital, and
  Bloemfontein the judicial capital.
- South Africa has the honourable distinction of being the
  only nuclear power voluntarily to dismantle its nuclear
  weapons programme.

- South Africa is a nonaligned state and is a member of the
  United Nations, the Commonwealth, the Southern African
  Development Community (SADC), the African Union, the
  World Trade Organisation and the Non-Aligned Movement.

FACT FILE » SOUTH AFRICA

Area	1 219 912 sq km
Population	47.9 million (estimated 2007)
Population density	39.2 per sq km
Population growth rate	1.56% (estimated 2007)
Urban population	57%
Literacy rate	77%
Capital city	Pretoria – administrative capital
	Cape Town – legislative capital
	Bloemfontein – judicial capital
Other principal cities	Johannesburg, Soweto, Durban,
	Port Elizabeth, East London
Coastline	2 955 km
National protected areas	6.5%
First democratic elections	27 April 1994
Official language	11 official languages
	(see The Life and Soul chapter)
Currency	Rand: R1 = 100 cents
Economic growth rate	5.0% (2006)
Annual GDP	US$255 billion (2006)
GDP per capita	US$5 300 (2006)
Global competitiveness ranking	44/117 (2007)
Information technology ranking	37/117 (2006)

- The judicial system is based on Roman Dutch and English Common Law and it operates through various court systems. Magistrates' courts deal with cases involving minor crimes and civil cases involving amounts of less than R100 000, while high courts deal with major civil and criminal cases and appeals from magistrates' courts. The Supreme Court is the final court of appeal for matters not relating to the Constitution and the Constitutional Court deals with matters relating to the Constitution. South Africa has independent watchdog organisations covering corruption, human rights, land claims and gender equality, and has a public protector.

THE ECONOMY

- South Africa is the economic powerhouse of Africa, contributing almost 30 per cent of the continent's GDP, and is the leader in manufacturing output, mineral production, electricity production, telecommunications use and financial flows. Globally, the economy was ranked the twenty-second largest according to GDP size in 2005.
- The economy is most often described as being a resource-based middle-income economy. South Africa is the world's

ABOVE *Through Sasol, a giant petrochemical corporation, South Africa has become the global leader in the production of synthetic liquid fuel and petrochemicals from coal.*

leading producer of platinum-group metals, gold, manganese and chrome, and is amongst the largest producers of low-grade coal, diamonds, titanium and uranium. The mining industry's contribution to GDP averages between 26 and 31 per cent.
- Besides an abundance of natural resources that have historically been the driving force, South Africa has well-developed financial, services and legal systems that support the large manufacturing base and an extensive transport and communications infrastructure.
- In the decade prior to the first democratic elections in 1994, economic growth averaged around 1 per cent. Since 1994, the economy has grown steadily and growth is currently at an annualised 5 per cent. The growth is due to a combination of excellent fiscal management, political and consumer confidence, a burgeoning middle class that translates into increased domestic demand, and a dramatic improvement in the tax collection system.

- The greater manufacturing sector contributes more than 20 per cent of GDP and is seen as a high-growth sector with substantial employment prospects. It comprises automobile assembly, metalwork, machine production, mineral processing, beverage and food processing, and the production of chemicals, fertilisers and textiles. South Africa is also a world leader in various specialised sectors, including the design and manufacture of types of mining equipment and the production of synthetic fuels.

- The major exports are mineral products, motor vehicles and car components. The major imported products are oil and petrochemicals, manufacturing equipment, motor vehicles and car components. The leading trading partners for exports are Japan, the USA and the UK. Imports come from Germany, China and the USA.

- The agricultural sector and its related industries contribute approximately 15 per cent to GDP and employ almost 10 per cent of the workforce. South Africa has a well-established commercial sector – the principal crops being maize, wheat, fruit, sugar cane and vegetables – and well-established beef, mutton, wool, poultry, dairy, logging and wine industries. It is a net exporter of food.

- Tourism presently contributes approximately 11 per cent of GDP and is the fastest-growing economic sector in the country. It is also a substantial provider of jobs, and one of the leading foreign exchange earners.

- In the world of high finance, South Africa is ranked along with Brazil, India and Malaysia in the pack of leading middle-income or 'emerging markets' for investment. The Johannesburg Securities Exchange (JSE) is ranked within the top 20 largest exchanges in the world by market capitalisation. The country has various other exchanges, including one for futures, bonds and commodities.

- Gauteng, which includes Johannesburg and its surrounds, is the economic hub. Producing almost 35 per cent of South Africa's GDP, the province is the leading financial and manufacturing centre. Other significant hubs include the Durban–Pinetown region in KwaZulu-Natal and the greater Cape Town area and the adjacent Overberg region in the Western Cape.

- With the unemployment rate at somewhere between 26 per cent and 40 per cent, South Africa also has a large

TOP *There have been an estimated 2.2 million AIDS-related deaths in South Africa – the first being in 1982. Approximately 5.5 million people currently live with HIV.*
ABOVE *The provinces of Mpumalanga and Limpopo have large citrus industries.*

informal economy, which operates outside the official tax collection, statistical and regulatory net. Comprising mostly traders and service providers, it provides millions of people living mainly in townships and informal settlements with a subsistence income.

- A central focus of government economic policy is Black Economic Empowerment (BEE). The strategy, while at times highly contentious, is crucial to correcting severe social and economic imbalances created during the apartheid years. Through legislation, a charter for each economic sector dictates percentage stakes that must be transferred into black ownership by given dates.

- Members of South Africa's burgeoning middle class are known locally as Black Diamonds. Presently consisting of 2.6 million people, this group is growing at almost 30 per cent per annum and now accounts for 28 per cent (2007) of the country's total purchasing power.

- In 2004, the government set itself the target of halving poverty and unemployment rates by 2014. To this end it introduced the Accelerated and Shared Growth Initiative for South Africa (Asgisa) which maps out the strategy and partnerships that will achieve the 6 per cent growth rates to fulfil these aims.

- In the Index of Economic Freedom 2007, South Africa ranks fifty-second out of 157 countries in the world. This is ahead of Italy (sixtieth), Brazil (seventieth), Greece (ninety-fourth), India (one hundred and fourth) and China (one hundred and nineteenth).

- According to the World Bank's annual *Doing Business* survey, South Africa fell six places in the global Ease of Business rankings, from twenty-ninth to thirty-fifth. This was in contrast to many of its major competitors in the developing world. China, India, Mauritius, Indonesia and Turkey, for example, all improved their rankings. In the World Economic Forum's Global Competitiveness Index for 2007, South Africa's ranking slipped from thirty-sixth to forty-fourth position.

- South Africa has become a leading global outsourcing service provider, with more than 500 call centres and help lines already established by international companies.

HEALTH

- The first AIDS death in South Africa was recorded in 1982. Since then there have been an estimated 2.2 million AIDS-related deaths and approximately 5.5 million people are currently living with HIV. There are an estimated one million AIDS orphans in South Africa.

- While South Africa has, since 1998, consistently appeared at or near the top of global AIDS-infection statistics, health officials believe the rate has peaked. In a report released in 2006, the National Department of Health estimated that 30.2 per cent of pregnant women were HIV positive. A more broadly based household survey found the HIV prevalence amongst those between 15 and 49 years old to be 16.2 per cent. The provinces of KwaZulu-Natal, Mpumalanga and Gauteng have the highest infection rates.

- South Africa has one of the world's largest antiretroviral (ARV) programmes in place. The recently released National Strategic Plan aims to cut new infections by 50 per cent and to bring treatment and support to at least 80 per cent of HIV positive people by 2011.

EDUCATION

- The education system in South Africa covers 13 years or grades and is divided into three bands. General Education and Training (GET) is compulsory and spans 10 years covering grade 0 (7 years of age) to grade 9. Further Education and Training (FET) is not compulsory. FET covers grades 10 to 12 and includes career-orientated education. Higher Education and Training (HET) incorporates tertiary education for undergraduate and postgraduate degrees. Only some schools in poverty-stricken regions offer free education.

- The public education system has almost 26 300 schools of various types, with approximately 380 000 educators teaching almost 12.5 million learners. South Africa also has a strong tradition of successful private schools with more than 1 000 registered private schools teaching almost 350 000 pupils.

- Higher education is catered for by 11 universities, five universities of technology, six comprehensive institutions and scores of teacher-training, nursing, agricultural and technical colleges. The University of South Africa (UNISA) is the largest correspondence university in the world, with more than 250 000 students.

- Although South Africa has one of the world's highest budgetary allocations to education (17.7 per cent in 2006), a legacy of apartheid is an illiteracy rate of almost 23 per cent of the adult population.

NATIONAL FLAG, SYMBOLS, ANTHEM AND MOTTO

- A new national flag was adopted in 1994 and flown for the first time on 10 May that year – at Nelson Mandela's presidential inauguration ceremony. While the six colours have no specific symbolism attached to them, the design showing a V form flowing into a horizontal band is symbolic of a diverse society converging onto a chosen single path towards unity.

- South Africa has a number of national symbols: the national fish is the galjoen (*Coracinus capensis*), the national bird is the Blue Crane (*Anthropoides paradisia*), the national animal is the springbok (*Antidorcas marsupialis*), the national tree is the yellowwood (*Podocarpus latifolius*) and the national flower is the king protea (*Protea cynaroides*).
- The national anthem is a combination of *Nkosi Sikelel' iAfrika* and the old apartheid-era anthem, *Die Stem van Suid-Afrika/The Call of South Africa*.
- The motto is 'Unity in Diversity', which comes from the Khoisan phrase *!ke e: /xarra //ke*, which means 'Diverse people unite'.

A brief history

Finds of some of the oldest human fossils, dating back more than three million years, have been made in South Africa. These were of *Australopithecus africanus*, an ancient human ancestor, while more recently, remains of *Homo sapiens*, dating back more than 50 000 years, have been found along the country's eastern coastline.

The earliest modern human inhabitants of southern Africa were the San and Khoikhoi people, collectively known as the Khoisan. The San people were hunter-gatherers who lived in small groups and roamed across the entire interior of the subcontinent, often moving with the large herds of wild animals once prevalent across the region. Because of the San people's lifestyle, few archaeological signs remain, other than an astonishing collection of rock art that dates back at least 25 000 years.

The Khoikhoi people, direct descendants of the San, moved southwards more than 2 000 years ago after acquiring herds of domestic stock from groups living further to the north. While the two groups continued to mix, the Khoikhoi people turned to a more pastoral lifestyle, settling along the western and southern coastal belts of South Africa.

South Africa's more recent history can be characterised by four notable periods.

ARRIVAL OF THE BANTU-SPEAKERS

Between the fourth and sixth centuries, Bantu-speaking people who originated from West Africa began arriving from Central and East Africa to settle in the region that is now South Africa. These movements took place in small waves over time, and with them the Bantu-speaking people displaced the San and Khoikhoi people wherever they encountered them. They brought new agricultural practices, large herds of domestic

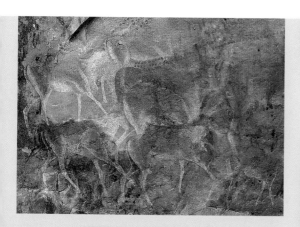

The San left an astonishing collection of rock art in places such as the Cederberg (above) and the Kamberg (right).

stock, political systems and, in later years, Iron Age technologies with them. Those that settled on the higher-lying central regions west of the uKhahlamba/Drakensberg mountain range were the ancestors of the Sotho, Tswana and Pedi people, while those who settled in the eastern regions below the uKhahlamba/Drakensberg mountain range and along the coastal strip of present-day South Africa were the ancestors of the Nguni cultures: the Xhosa, Zulu, Pondo and Swazi.

COLONIALISM

This period began with the arrival of the first Dutch settlers in 1652 and covered more than 250 years of expansionism across the subcontinent by European settlers, predominately of Dutch and British descent. The process included frequent frontier wars between black African groups and settlers, and two major settler wars between the British and descendants of the Dutch (known as Boers). Two crucial events, the discovery of diamonds and that of gold, took place during this period. By the early 1900s, almost all tribal groups of black people had in some way been forced from their traditional lands and, for the most part, been politically disenfranchised.

APARTHEID

The ravages of colonialism created the platform for the horrors of apartheid to take hold when the Afrikaner-dominated National Party took control of South Africa in 1948. Based on prejudice and discrimination, the new government institutionalised its racist perception of South Africa's future through the policy of separate development for the different racial groups. Characterised by the introduction of a raft of severely discriminatory legislation aimed at promoting white dominance, these laws impacted on the population across the political, social and economic spectrums.

The system was enforced by a bloc of cunning white voters and a well-oiled bureaucracy, which were brutally aided by police and military forces that openly sided with the

RIGHT *The colonial era was characterised by frequent wars. Here, a grave site and a British war memorial commemorate the Battle of Isandlwana (1879), where the British army suffered its heaviest defeat by the Zulus.*

regime of the day. Together, these constituencies set about ensuring the majority of the black population was excluded from South African life as they attempted to dump almost 80 per cent of the population into a mere 13 per cent of the land. Known as homelands or 'bantustans', the overcrowded tracts of land making up this small percentage were the most underdeveloped areas in South Africa and represented the poorest agricultural potential.

The 1970s and 1980s were the darkest days of apartheid. During this period South Africa was, in fact, at war with itself as the liberation movements, both internally and externally, rallied the people of South Africa to revolt and most of the world to stand up against the apartheid system. While the fight against apartheid was successful, for the foreseeable future, the grim reality is that this era is likely to remain the period that stands out in South Africa's history.

THE RAINBOW NATION

Decades of apartheid built up widespread polarity, hatred and bitterness, and because of this, few people the world

over gave South Africa much chance of a smooth and peaceful settlement. Despite the divisions and animosities and amidst widespread fears amongst the minority, South Africa nonetheless achieved the near impossible with the dawn of the Rainbow Nation. While the struggle had played the decisive role of severely weakening the government of the day, the momentum for a new South Africa came with the unbanning of the liberation movements and the release of Nelson Mandela and all other political prisoners in the early 1990s. Despite fears of a right-wing backlash and a military coup, the true leaders of the new South Africa forged ahead with the drafting of a new constitution and preparations for the country's first free and fair elections. Since that euphoric day in early 1994, South Africa has scarcely looked back.

While the white leadership of the apartheid era can take a smidgen of credit for at least realising that the time of the sin of apartheid was over, the true acknowledgement for South Africa's peaceful transition must go to the majority of the black population. The reach of reconciliation that has come from these communities and their powers of forgiveness have been truly remarkable. Failures have certainly occurred and challenges there are aplenty, but, in general, South Africa has become an example to the rest of the world of how unity can be forged out of diversity.

A TIMELINE OF SOUTH AFRICAN HISTORY

12th–14th centuries: Most of South Africa has been settled by Bantu-speaking groups living mostly in organised chiefdoms. The Iron Age civilisation of Mapungubwe, the largest and most complex kingdom on the subcontinent, is at the height of its power.

1488–97: The Portuguese explorer Bartolomeu Dias becomes the first European to enter South African waters when he rounds the southern tip of Africa in 1488. The Portuguese captain Vasco da Gama lands along the present-day KwaZulu-Natal coast in 1497 while en route to India.

1652–57: In 1652, 90 men – under the leadership of Jan van Riebeeck and representing the Dutch East India Company – land at the Cape of Good Hope. They establish a fort and supply base for the growing trade route from Europe to the East. In 1657, the first nine members of the party are given farming rights in the Cape. In the following decades, Dutch, German and French Huguenot settlers establish further settlements.

Late 1600s: The Khoikhoi people rise against the Dutch settlers as the settlers begin claiming land in the hinterland beyond present-day Cape Town.

1779–81: The first frontier war between the Dutch and the Xhosa is fought as European settlements extend eastwards, displacing Xhosa chiefdoms. Another eight frontier wars are fought, the last in the 1870s, as settlers continue to take land from the Xhosa.

1795–1816: In 1795, France conquers the Netherlands, resulting in Britain's annexing the Cape Colony to keep it out of French control. The British return it to the Dutch in 1803 but retake it in 1806, before it is finally ceded to them in 1816.

Early 1800s: External and internal political tensions, exacerbated by severe drought conditions, result in major disputes and conflicts between the Nguni groups living in the eastern regions of present-day South Africa. Known as the *Mfecane* or 'The Crushing' to the Nguni people, and the *Difaqane* or 'Scattering' to the Sotho people, this period lasts almost four decades and results in many groups and chiefdoms moving to settle further north.

1816–28: Shaka becomes king of the Zulu people in 1816, and the Zulu kingdom achieves political and military prominence. The Xhosa and Swazi people, and various smaller groups, are forced from the region that is present-day KwaZulu-Natal. Shaka is assassinated in 1828 by his two half-brothers, and one of them, Dingane, becomes king.

1820: More than 5 000 British settlers arrive, and they settle mostly along the southern coast and in the Eastern Cape. This influx of English-speaking people would lead to many conflicts between the Afrikaners and the English.

1833–34: The British abolish the slave trade and all slaves within the Cape Colony are freed.

1835–40: With the ending of the slave trade and in order to avoid British colonial rule, approximately 10 000 disgruntled farmers, or Boers, leave the Cape Colony by ox-wagon and head north and northeast on the Great Trek. Known as Voortrekkers, they displace various Bantu-speaking peoples along the way, and settle in Natal, the Orange Free State and the Transvaal. The most famous battle is that of Blood River, where the Boers defeat the Zulu army on the banks of the Mulaudzi River in 1838.

1843–59: The British annex Natal in 1843, but recognise the independence of the Boer Republics by granting self-government to the Transvaal in 1852 and the Orange Free State in 1854. By now most black Africans have lost their traditional lands.

1860: The first Indian labourers arrive in Durban to work the sugar plantations established by the British. Mahondas Gandhi arrives in 1893 to serve as a legal counsel. By 1900, more than 100 000 Indians are living in Natal.

1866–71: The first diamond is discovered in 1866 on a farm south of Kimberley and the first major diamond pipe is unearthed on the present-day site of Kimberley in 1870, setting off a mining rush. Through deals they make with the local Griqua leaders, the British take control of Kimberley in 1871 by incorporating it into the Cape Colony.

1872: The British government grants autonomy to the Cape Colony.

1877: Britain annexes the Transvaal.

1879: In January, the Battle of Isandlwana takes place and the British army suffers its heaviest defeat at the hands of the Zulu army under the leadership of King Cetshwayo. The Battle of Rorke's Drift takes place nearby, where just more than 100 British soldiers hold out in a mission station and field hospital against thousands of Zulu soldiers. Eleven Victoria Crosses are awarded, the most ever given by the British in a single battle. By mid-year, and after numerous battles, the British defeat the Zulus in a final battle at Ulundi. This ends the Zulu kingdom's era of dominance and brings Natal under full control of the British.

1880–83: The Boers rise up against the British in the first Anglo-Boer War and defeat them after a resounding victory in the Battle of Majuba Hill in 1881. An agreement is signed which hands Transvaal back to the Boers. It achieves independence as the *Zuid Afrikaansche Republiek* (ZAR), with Paul Kruger becoming President in 1883.

1886: The Witwatersrand gold fields are discovered, triggering both a major rush for gold and a further influx of Europeans into South Africa. While the twin discoveries of diamonds and gold begin South Africa's industrialisation process and catapult the country into a global position, they also lead to the introduction of practices such as the hostel complexes for cheap black migrant labour, the pass law system and job discrimination based on colour. These will set the tone for South Africa's divided and racist political and social future.

1895–98: In 1895, Cecil John Rhodes, leader of the Cape Colony, plots to overthrow the ZAR with the launching of the Jameson Raid. The raid is a failure and the raiders are captured by the Boers. This event and decisions by the British government to demand voting rights for foreigners and to send reinforcement troops to South Africa are precursors to the beginning of the second Anglo-Boer War.

1899: The second Anglo-Boer War begins when the ZAR and the Orange Free State declare war on Britain.

1902: After a protracted campaign of guerrilla tactics fought by the Boers and a responsive scorched-earth policy by the British, the war ends with the Boers surrendering and signing the Treaty of Vereeniging. Transvaal is granted the status of a self-governing colony of the British Empire in 1906, and the Orange Free State gains the same status in 1907.

1910: The Union of South Africa is formed between the former British colonies of the Cape and Natal and the Boer republics of Transvaal and Orange Free State. It becomes a self-governing dominion of the British Empire, and its constitution ensures the exclusion of voting rights for the black population living outside the Cape.

1912: The South African Native National Congress, later to be renamed the African National Congress (ANC), is founded in Bloemfontein. Its aims are the breaking down of the separate development policies of the Union and the achievement of parliamentary representation for the black population.

1913: The Land Act, which prevents black people from buying or leasing land outside designated black tribal 'reserves' (except in the Cape Province), is introduced. It is the first institutionalised act restricting black people to living on approximately 13 per cent of the land.

1914–18: After splitting from the South African Party (SAP), the National Party (NP) is founded in 1914 by J.B.M. Hertzog to promote the interests of the Afrikaner people. Four years later, the secretive Broederbond (brotherhood) is formed to further enhance the Afrikaner cause.

1919: Jan Smuts becomes Prime Minster of the Union. He will again become Prime Minster in 1939.

1921: The Communist Party of South Africa is formed with a predominately white membership.

1935–36: The Union constitution is amended to remove all voting rights for black people living in the Cape.

1946: In 1946, J.B. Marks leads more than 100 000 black miners in strike action. This contributes to the banning of the Communist Party in 1950.

1948–50: The NP, under the leadership of D.F. Malan, takes power in 1948 and introduces the policies of apartheid (separateness). In 1949, the Mixed Marriages Act prohibiting cross-cultural marriages is introduced, and in 1950 the Group Areas Act segregating residential areas into white and black areas, and the Population Registration Act classifying people according to race, come into law.

1951–52: The first steps towards the establishment of black 'homelands', or 'bantustans', are taken with the introduction of the Bantu Authorities Act in 1951. The Native Laws

Under the Native Resettlement Act, the first 60 families in Sophiatown, Johannesburg, were forcibly removed from their homes in February 1955.

Amendment Act, or the hated Pass Laws (as it becomes known), comes into law a year later and forces black people to carry identification papers with them at all times. In effect, black people cannot leave the designated homelands without a permit and cannot move about urban areas without being able to produce a 'pass' to the authorities. An act is passed in 1956 to deny black people the right to a court appeal against being forcibly removed from an area.

1952: In response to the policies of the NP, the ANC, together with the South African Indian Congress, launches the Defiance Campaign, led by Nelson Mandela, which promotes peaceful civil disobedience against South Africa's racist laws.

1953: The Separate Amenities Act forcing segregation in all public amenities and public buildings and on all forms of public transport is passed. The law is publicly proclaimed with 'Europeans Only' and 'Non-Europeans Only' signs in all public places. The Bantu Education Act introduces separate education with black people being taught a curriculum that in the words of Hendrik Verwoerd, its architect, will suit the 'nature and requirements of the black people'. The Native Labour Act prohibits any form of protest and strike action by black people while at the work place. Also in 1953, the Communist Party reforms as the South African Communist Party; it operates as an underground movement.

1955: A gathering of more than 3 000 people from various political and civic resistance movements adopts the Freedom Charter at the Congress of the People in Kliptown, outside Johannesburg. The document promotes the vision of a free and democratic state.

1956: Opposition activists and 156 ANC leaders are arrested and charged with treason. They are all acquitted in 1960, although many are served with house arrest and other restrictive orders.

1959: Dissatisfied members of the ANC break away to form the Pan-Africanist Congress (PAC). Under the leadership of Robert Sobukwe, the group rallies under the banner of 'Africa for the Africans'. The Extension of University Education Act is passed, banning black students from attending white universities. The formalisation of the 'homelands' policy

ABOVE *This plaque, outside the Hector Pieterson Museum in Soweto, commemorates the 1976 Soweto Uprisings.*
LEFT *The District Six Museum in Cape Town.*

takes another major step with the Promotion of Bantu Self-Government Act. It classifies black people into eight ethnic groups and promotes the policy of 'Separate Development', whereby each group belongs to a quasi-independent and self-governing homeland.

1960: During mass demonstrations, 69 black people are killed and more than 180 wounded by the police in Sharpeville, outside Johannesburg, while peacefully protesting against the Pass Laws. The government bans the ANC and the PAC and detains numerous leaders. These events lead to the groups adopting armed resistance. Chief Albert Lutuli, president-general of the ANC, becomes the first South African to be awarded the Nobel Peace Prize.

1961: South Africa becomes a republic and, amidst growing local and international criticism of its policies, withdraws from the Commonwealth. The ANC launches its military wing, Umkhonto we Sizwe (Spear of the Nation), with Nelson Mandela as its first commander-in-chief, and begins attacks on government installations and economic targets.

1963–64: The police raid a farm in Rivonia outside Johannesburg and discover crucial documents linking the leadership of the ANC and Umkhonto we Sizwe to sabotage attacks. Numerous leaders – including Nelson Mandela, Walter Sisulu and Govan Mbeki – are arrested and put on trial. Known as the Rivonia Trialists, they are found guilty and sentenced to life imprisonment in 1964. Those who escape

arrest, most notably Oliver Tambo, go into exile and lead the ANC from abroad.

1966: Prime Minister Hendrik Verwoerd is assassinated while addressing parliament. He is succeeded by B.J. Vorster.

1967: The Terrorism Act is introduced, which allows for detention without trial over an indefinite period. The Bureau of State Security (BOSS) is formed and is tasked with managing the internal security affairs of South Africa.

1969: The South African Students Organisation (SASO) is formed after a number of leaders break away from the National Union of South African Students (NUSAS). In later years and under the leadership of Steve Biko, the ideology of Black Consciousness is introduced to masses of black school pupils.

1970: The Bantu Homelands Citizenship Act removes citizenship rights from all black people living in South Africa, irrespective of where they were born. The act also forces them to become citizens of a homeland, depending on their ethnic classification.

1976: In June, the Soweto Uprising begins. What begins as student protests over education issues rapidly develops into nationwide anti-government riots. Almost 1 000 protestors are killed by police during the year, and thousands more escape South Africa to undergo military training abroad. In the same year, the Transkei becomes the first 'homeland' state to take 'independence'. Although never recognised outside

ABOVE *A typical sign enforcing segregation that appeared all over South Africa between 1948 and 1990.*

RIGHT *The Hector Pieterson Memorial in Soweto, Johannesburg.*

South Africa, the 'homelands' of Ciskei, Bophuthatswana and Venda follow suit.

1977: Steve Biko is killed by security police after being heavily tortured in detention.

1983: After a mass gathering of anti-apartheid and community organisations, the United Democratic Front (UDF) is formed to serve as an umbrella body for a renewed wave of nationwide protest and strike action against the government.

1984: A new tricameral parliament is introduced and the Constitution is changed to allow limited access to government by coloured and Asian communities. Black people remain totally disenfranchised. Later in the year, Bishop Desmond Tutu is awarded the Nobel Peace Prize (see page 64).

1985–86: Most township communities are in open revolt and a State of Emergency is introduced. Internationally, political, economic, cultural and sport sanctions against South Africa are put in place. By 1986, talks between certain government members, the opposition, the business sector and the ANC in exile have begun.

1989: P.W. Botha is forced from his position as President and is replaced by F.W. de Klerk. De Klerk meets with Mandela, and many ANC activists are freed.

1990–93: In 1990, the ANC, PAC and many other anti-apartheid groups are unbanned and Mandela is released after spending 27 years in jail. This heralds the start of multiparty talks and the abolition of all apartheid laws in 1991. In 1993,

agreement is reached on a new interim Constitution. During the same year, Mandela and De Klerk are awarded the Nobel Peace Prize (see page 62).

1994: The first nonracial national elections are held, and the ANC gains 63 per cent of the vote. On 10 May, Mandela becomes President and he forms a Government of National Unity. South Africa is welcomed back into the United Nations fold and rejoins the Commonwealth.

1996: Under the chairmanship of Desmond Tutu, the Truth and Reconciliation Commission (TRC) begins hearings on human rights abuses and crimes by both government and liberation forces during the apartheid era (see page 65). The new democratic Constitution is formally adopted.

1999: The ANC wins the second post-apartheid national elections and Thabo Mbeki takes over as President.

2003: Walter Sisulu, a key ANC leader and struggle stalwart, dies at the age of 90.

2004: The ANC wins national elections with almost 70 per cent of the vote. Thabo Mbeki begins his second and last five-year term.

2007: Jacob Zuma wins the nomination to succeed Thabo Mbeki as head of the ANC.

2008: Because of a bitter feud within the ANC, Thabo Mbeki is recalled as President and resigns his position. Kgalema Motlanthe is installed as caretaker President until the next elections in early 2009.

Nobel laureates

South Africa has eight Nobel laureates: Max Theiler (Medicine, in 1951); Albert Luthuli (Peace, in 1960); Allan Cormack (Medicine, in 1979); Desmond Tutu (Peace, in 1984); Nadine Gordimer (Literature, in 1991); Nelson Mandela (Peace, in 1993); F.W. de Klerk (Peace, in 1993 – shared with Nelson Mandela) and J.M. Coetzee (Literature, in 2003). Of these eight esteemed South Africans, two individuals stand out. They have been the leading role players in the transformation of South Africa from a pariah state during the apartheid era to a fledgling democracy that is now universally acknowledged.

NELSON ROLIHLAHLA MANDELA

What more is there to say about this incredible man? He is regarded throughout the world as one of the greatest statesmen of all time and revered at home across the political spectrum as the guiding force behind the new South Africa. Such is Mandela's standing today that wherever he may be, world leaders, politicians, film stars, sports heroes and rock stars seek his company and endorsement.

His unwavering and selfless commitment to ridding South Africa of racism and oppression, and replacing them with a free and democratic order, has been a lifetime's work. And no matter what his role – as leader of the freedom struggle, political prisoner, politician, president or elder citizen – Mandela has always shown courageous leadership, deep understanding and immense wisdom.

But he has not always been accorded such admiration. For 27 years, while it locked him away on Robben Island, the apartheid regime portrayed him as public enemy number one, and numerous conservative global leaders, including those from the USA and the UK during the 1980s, offered him or his causes little or no support. Instead, they readily went along with the South African government, tagging him as a dangerous 'terrorist', and they refused to support the sanctions movement.

Mandela has made a great many celebrated speeches in his time, but the one many regard as his most inspirational was given from the dock during the Rivonia Trial. It ended with these words:

I have fought against white domination, and I have fought against black domination. I have cherished the ideal of a democratic and free society in which all persons live together in harmony and with equal opportunities. It is an ideal which I hope to live for and to achieve. But if needs be, it is an ideal for which I am prepared to die.

After Mandela's release from prison in 1990, it was without doubt his inspirational leadership qualities that played the vital role in ensuring South Africa's smooth transformation. His message of reconciliation and forgiveness, dispensed with such humility and charisma, became the benchmark in all negotiations during his term as the first democratically elected President of South Africa.

Some important dates in the life of Nelson Mandela:

1918: Born on 18 July in Mvezo, Eastern Cape.

1940: While studying for a BA degree, he is expelled from Fort Hare University for participating in political activities and organising strike action. He completes his studies through correspondence, and receives a law degree from the University of the Witwatersrand.

1942: Mandela joins the African National Congress (ANC).

1944: With Walter Sisulu and Oliver Tambo, Mandela forms the Youth League of the ANC (ANCYL) as a means of expressing their more radical approach to national self-determination.

1947: Mandela is elected secretary of the ANCYL.

1950: Mandela is elected to the National Executive Committee (NEC) of the ANC.

1952: Tambo and Mandela start the first black law firm in South Africa. Mandela becomes deputy president of the ANC, and is elected to organise the national Defiance Campaign.

1956: Along with 156 other anti-apartheid activists, Mandela is arrested and charged with high treason.

1958: Mandela marries Nomzamo Winnifred Madikizela.

ABOVE *Defendants Moses Kotane (left) and Nelson Mandela leave a courtroom in Pretoria during the Treason Trial, 1958.*

1961: Mandela and the other activists are found not guilty, but Mandela is served with a banning order. Umkhonto we Sizwe (Spear of the Nation) is formed with Mandela as its first commander-in-chief. In a keynote speech given in Pieter-maritzburg, Mandela challenges the government to hold a convention for a new constitution. Authorities issue a warrant for his arrest for breaking his banning order.

1962: Mandela addresses a conference in Addis Ababa after being smuggled out of South Africa. While abroad he organises guerrilla training for members of Umkhonto we Sizwe. Shortly after returning to South Africa he is arrested and receives a five-year prison sentence for breaking his banning order and inciting people to strike.

1963–64: The Rivonia trials take place and Mandela and eight others receive life sentences for plotting to overthrow the state. They are imprisoned on Robben Island, a maximum-security prison 11 km offshore of Cape Town.

1970s: Mandela is offered a remission of sentence and a home in the Transkei if he accepts the regime's homeland policy. He refuses.

Early 1980s: Mandela is transferred from Robben Island to Pollsmoor Prison in Cape Town. The internationally organised 'Release Mandela Campaign' takes place around the globe. Mandela is again offered his freedom, this time in exchange for renouncing violence, but turns down the offer.

1988: Mandela is moved to Victor Verster Prison in Paarl where he is allowed to live in a private house. Certain government and opposition party members engage with him in 'behind-the-scenes' talks.

1990: After serving 27 years in prison, Mandela is released on 11 February.

1991: Mandela becomes head of the ANC and leads the ANC delegation in talks with the government for a new constitution.

1993: Mandela wins the Nobel Peace Prize and accepts it on behalf of all those who have struggled for peace and democracy in South Africa.

1994: On 10 May, Mandela is inaugurated as President of South Africa.

1998: Two years after divorcing his wife Winnie, Mandela marries Graça Machel on his 80th birthday.

1999: Mandela hands over the presidency to Thabo Mbeki and retires from active politics.

2008: Mandela turns 90 years of age.

ARCHBISHOP EMERITUS DESMOND MPILO TUTU

While Desmond Tutu may not enjoy the same level of global recognition as Nelson Mandela, he certainly shares equal status with him at home and in many parts of Africa. In fact, during the 1980s and some of the darkest days of apartheid, Tutu became the face of the activist struggle, carrying the hopes and dreams of a divided nation with him. With most of the ANC's senior leaders either in prison or in exile, Tutu was one of a number of people who stepped in to fill the leadership vacuum.

It was a role he played with immense courage and vision, and, ultimately, with stunning success. More often than not, it was Tutu who was found at the head of public marches, leading defiance campaigns or taking government politicians and their international sympathisers to task. Because of the very visible and effective role he played, he soon became unpopular amongst the majority of white South Africans and government supporters. Despite being faced with spiralling unrest across South Africa, and the growing brutality being meted out by the armed forces, these constituencies tried to convince the world that it was not appropriate for a clergyman to be a leader of dissent.

Today, most of those opponents and doubters are converts. His appeal is now broad-based, stretching across racial, religious and political lines, and he has become one of South Africa's all-time favourite icons. While his coining of the phrase 'Rainbow Nation' – now universally used to describe the new multiracial South Africa – and his charming sense of humour have no doubt helped to win him many fans, his honesty, principled sense of justice and support for the downtrodden single him out as a leader with immense integrity. Over a decade into the new order, Tutu remains a respected voice of reason, and a strong critic of inefficient, corrupt and wayward public figures.

Some important dates in the life of Desmond Tutu:

1931: Born on 7 October in Klerksdorp, in present-day North West province.

1954: Tutu graduates with a Diploma in Teaching from a college in Pretoria. He later receives a BA degree from the University of South Africa.

1955: On 2 July, he marries Leah Nomalizo Shinxani.

1960–61: After training at St Peter's Theological College in Johannesburg, Tutu is ordained as a deacon. A year later, he is ordained as a priest.

1962–67: Tutu heads for England, where he studies theology at King's College, London, and receives his Master of Theology degree. In 1967, he returns to South Africa to teach theology.

1972: Tutu leaves for England as Associate Director of the Theological Fund of the World Council of Churches.

1975: Tutu is appointed Dean of St Mary's Cathedral in Johannesburg.

1976–78: In 1976, he is appointed as the Bishop of Lesotho and in 1978 as the first black General Secretary of the South African Council of Churches. In 1977, he speaks at the funeral of Steve Biko – this is a political turning point for Tutu.

1979: The government revokes Tutu's passport because of his numerous overseas visits, during which he consistently lobbies against the South African government and calls for economic sanctions.

1982: In recognition for the role he is playing in the anti-apartheid movement, Columbia University awards Tutu his first honorary degree.

1984: Tutu is awarded the Nobel Prize in Peace and is elected as the first black Anglican Bishop of Johannesburg.

1986: He becomes Archbishop of Cape Town when he is elected to the highest position in the Anglican Church in South Africa.

1995: Tutu is appointed Chairperson of the Truth and Reconciliation Commission (TRC) (see page 65), which investigates apartheid-era crimes.

1996: In a decision to devote all his time to the TRC, Tutu retires as Archbishop of Cape Town.

2004: Tutu is appointed Visiting Professor of King's College in London.

2006: The Indian government awards Tutu the prestigious Gandhi Peace Prize.

2007: Along with various other highly respected retired global leaders, Tutu convenes The Elders, an advisory body to assist with solving the world's major problems. Tutu is Chairperson.

TRUTH AND RECONCILIATION COMMISSION

The Truth and Reconciliation Commission (TRC) was established to investigate crimes and acts of political murder and sabotage committed by the various arms of the South African security apparatus, as well as the liberation forces, during the apartheid era. Because many people were killed under mysterious circumstances, assassinated or simply disappeared, the work of the Commission was to unravel these incidents and, in so doing, become part of the forgiveness and reconciliation process in South Africa.

It was a monumental task, and because of its sensitive and politicised nature, much of the Commission's work

ABOVE *Desmond Tutu was a hugely influential leader during the days of apartheid and has since become one of South Africa's most respected icons.*

has been criticised by both sides of the political divide. Supporters of the old regime point out that many incidents of sabotage committed by ANC guerrillas were never investigated, while opponents of apartheid argue that none of the then-government's leaders have been prosecuted for their crimes, and that the TRC has been lenient on the foot soldiers who have appeared before it. For further reading, go to www.doj.gov.za/trc

PLATEAUS
and PLAINS

*S*outh Africa is recognised the world over for its rich and varied mineral deposits, gold, platinum and diamonds in particular. But the occurrence of these riches is not merely coincidental: they indicate a unique geology and are a product of ancient forces and processes that go back over 3.5 billion years. These involve various ice ages, continental drift and other tectonic movements, the influence of ocean flows, and aeons of changing weather and erosion patterns. Today, although well worn and weathered with a fascinating array of geological forms, the region remains relatively stable.

PREVIOUS PAGES *This kokerboom forest occurs in the mountains just outside the Great Karoo town of Calvinia.*

ABOVE *This striking massif is part of the Waterberg mountains, which rise to the northwest of Pretoria.*

Topography

The origin of South Africa's topography dates back almost 3.6 billion years, after the earth started cooling sufficiently for landmasses to form. The oldest rocks – igneous and sedimentary types that underlie the subcontinent – are found in the eastern regions around the town of Barberton. In these formations remnants of blue-green algae, some of the earliest traces of life on earth, have also been found.

Subsequently, and over millions of years, tumultuous forces originating from the earth's core have deposited further layers of volcanic rock, both beneath the earth's crust and – as lava flows – above the surface, over older layers. Weathering by water, wind and sand has created the sedimentary layers that have been compacted into conglomerates, sandstones and shales. Plate tectonics and shifting continents gave rise to Africa approximately 135 million years ago, and then changing climates and cataclysmic folding also played their roles, with the formation of mountain ranges and the creation of vast inland 'seas'. Those interested in a detailed explanation on southern Africa's formation can read *The Story of Earth and Life – A Southern African Perspective* by Terence McCarthy and Bruce Rubidge.

Seven biomes

A biome, or biotic community, is a collection of plant and animal species that survive in a broadly defined ecological zone or geographical area. Biomes are characterised by having a dominant vegetation type, and all species that live within a biome have adapted to the climatic conditions associated with the biome. There are seven terrestrial biomes recognised in South Africa.

SAVANNAH BIOME

The largest biome in South Africa covers most of the western and northern regions, the Lowveld and the Kruger National Park and extends into northern KwaZulu-Natal. Savannahs occur in various forms – woodland, bushveld and shrubveld – but all have grass cover at ground level.

ABOVE *Situated along the coast in the Western Cape, the De Hoop Nature Reserve is a typical example of the fynbos biome.*

69

South Africa's varied topography

ABOVE *This plaque at Cape Agulhas marks the southernmost tip of South Africa and the continent of Africa.*

- A low-lying coastal plain extends inland between 50 and 200 km, and runs the entire length of the southern and eastern coastline. It is widest in the south and narrowest in the east.
- Further north, a low-lying region (mostly below 1 000 m) – known as the Lowveld – runs along South Africa's entire border with Mozambique.
- Highland regions rise up from the coastal plain and extend towards the interior of South Africa. Known as the Great Escarpment, this highland region extends almost the entire length of the country from the northeast to the southwest. It is dominated by the uKhahlamba/Drakensberg mountain range, along the border with Lesotho. The mountains are the remnants of extensively weathered, massive flows of lava, which occurred almost 200 million years ago.
- Dropping away from the Great Escarpment on the inland side, a region of medium altitude (1 000 to 2 000 m on average) is known as the Central Plateau or Highveld.

- The central and western interior comprises a lower lying bowl – higher lying in the east than in the west – that is mostly semidesert sandveld. Formed approximately 60 million years ago, this is often referred to as the Kalahari Basin, which is part of the largest mass of unbroken sand that exists on the planet. The Kalahari is characterised by nutrient-poor soils.
- In the western, southern and eastern regions of the Cape are the Cape Fold mountain ranges, which began forming almost 500 million years ago. They extend no further than approximately 150 km inland. Well-known ranges include the Cederberg, Swartberg, Hex River mountains and Outeniqua mountains.
- The Little Karoo and the Great Karoo lie within the rain shadow of the Cape Fold mountains and the uKhahlamba/Drakensberg range respectively. These rain-shadow regions have a drier climate with various semidesert vegetation types.
- Mafadi Peak (3 446 m) in the central uKhahlamba/Drakensberg is the highest point in South Africa, while Thaba Ntlenyana (3 482 m), immediately across the border in Lesotho, is the highest point in southern Africa.
- Lesotho, lying in the central regions, is completely surrounded by South Africa.
- South Africa possesses two small islands, Marion Island (290 sq km) and Prince Edward Island (46 sq km), that lie 1 920 km off the southern tip of Africa. The islands were annexed by South Africa in 1947.
- The main river system is the Orange–Vaal system, which is 2 188 km long and drains off the Lesotho highlands. The Limpopo River, which drains off the Highveld, is the next longest. Smaller systems include the uThukela, Breede, Sundays, Fish and Berg rivers.
- The Thukela Falls in the uKhahlamba/Drakensberg range is the highest waterfall in the country, dropping 948 m over five consecutive drops.
- Cape Agulhas is the southernmost point of South Africa and the African continent.

GRASSLAND BIOME

This lies predominately on the Highveld and in parts of KwaZulu-Natal and the Eastern Cape. There are two broad but distinct categories of grasses: sweet grasses have a low fibre content and are generally more palatable to wildlife and livestock, while sour grasses have a higher fibre content and are less palatable to grazers.

FOREST BIOME

The smallest of the biomes, the forest biome is found patchily along the Garden Route, in parts of KwaZulu-Natal and the Lowveld and along the Great Escarpment. Forests occur in the higher-rainfall areas from sea level to mid-altitude. They are characterised by a canopy cover with layers of different vegetation types below.

ABOVE *An ostrich on its nest in the grasslands of the lAi-lAis/ Richtersveld Transfrontier Park.*

FYNBOS BIOME

This biome comprises part of the Cape Floral Kingdom, the smallest and richest of the six recognised kingdoms of plants. It covers much of the Western Cape and stretches towards Port Elizabeth in the Eastern Cape. Fynbos plants are characterised as tough with small and leathery leaves, and 68 per cent of the plants in this kingdom are endemic.

SUCCULENT KAROO BIOME

This biome occurs on the flat, arid plains immediately to the north of the Cape Fold mountain ranges, where winter rainfall is low. The biome has an extremely rich diversity of plants for such arid conditions and it has a high number of rare and threatened species. Associated with the geographical region of the Little Karoo, this biome also extends along the northern reaches of the West Coast up towards the IAi-IAis/Richtersveld Transfrontier Park. The vegetation is dominated by dwarf succulent shrubs.

NAMA KAROO BIOME

Characterised by grassy shrubveld, this biome covers large parts of the Great Karoo, extending into the Northern Cape and eastwards towards the central regions of the country, between the altitudes of 500 m and 2 000 m.

DESERT BIOME

This is found in the harsh semidesert conditions along the Orange River and in the IAi-IAis/Richtersveld Transfrontier Park. Summer rainfall occurs, but is erratic and the region has long spells of little or no precipitation. Vegetation is sparse and is dominated by annual grasses and succulent shrubs. (Some texts indicate that these regions fall into the Nama Karoo biome. They refer instead to a thicket biome – in parts of the Eastern Cape, particularly the Baviaanskloof and the Addo region – as the seventh biome.)

Climatic patterns

Three distinct climatic patterns occur in different parts of South Africa. These are influenced primarily by latitude, topography and the major currents in the two surrounding oceans – the Atlantic and Indian oceans.

South Africa lies within a subtropical zone characterised by high atmospheric pressures. It is influenced by cold westerly air movements coming from the polar regions (winter) and warmer air movements coming from the northeast (summer). The highland regions of the Great Escarpment act as a barrier to the movement of air further inland. On the Atlantic Ocean side, the cold Benguela Current comes up from the Antarctic and flows northwards along the west coast. The air flowing off the cold ocean towards the warmer land yields very little rain, but plenty of fog. In contrast, on the Indian Ocean side, the Agulhas Current flows southwards along the east coast, bring-

ing warm water from the tropics. The air movements over the warm ocean are a major influence on the substantially higher rainfall patterns in the east of South Africa. The average annual rainfall for the country is 464 mm, which is well below the global average. Parts of the far west get less than 200 mm, and a few places in the east receive 1 500 mm.

Because of their southerly latitude, Cape Town and the western and southern regions of the Cape experience a Mediterranean-type climate, with cold and wet winter weather from May through to September. The warm summer period from October to April is mostly dry. The average annual rainfall in Cape Town is 520 mm. Summer temperatures average 22 °C, with winter temperatures averaging 11 °C.

A feature of the Cape summer is the southeasterly winds – known to the locals as The Cape Doctor – that can, at times, reach gale force. During midwinter, snowfalls occur on many of the higher peaks of the Cape Fold mountain ranges.

For the rest of South Africa, apart from the eastern coastal strip, the climate is temperate. The winter period from May to late September is dry and cool, while the summer period is wet and warm, with thunderstorms an almost daily occurrence. In Johannesburg, the annual rainfall averages 780 mm, summer temperatures average 22 °C and winter temperatures drop to an average of 10 °C.

The eastern coastal strip of KwaZulu-Natal running along the Indian Ocean has a subtropical climate with rain falling

ABOVE Storm clouds roll off the Indian Ocean, bringing rain to the Wild Coast region in the Eastern Cape.

throughout the year. The summers are hot and humid and the winters are mild. In Durban, the average annual rainfall is 1 009 mm, and summer temperatures average 25 °C, while winter averages a mild 17 °C.

The coldest temperatures (as low as -15 °C) are regularly recorded in the Sutherland region of the central Karoo and the Molteno region of the Eastern Cape. The warmest temperatures (more than 50 °C) occur along the Orange River in the Northern Cape. Frost occurs in the high-altitude regions during the winter months.

en ROUTE

South Africa has a well-developed road network with more than 750 000 km of roads. The largest in Africa, this network includes almost 10 000 km of national highways and freeways, 56 000 km of paved provincial roads, more than 300 000 km of well-maintained gravel roads and 2 500 km of toll roads. The national roads linking the major cities and towns are marked on maps in blue, for example N1 or N2. Main provincial roads are marked in yellow with the R designation, such as R62 or R101, and major freeways heading in and out of the cities are marked as M1 or M5, for example.

Although the rail service does not cover every corner of the country, all the major cities and larger towns are linked by the national railways, and there are a few private rail operators that cover the more popular routes. There are also numerous private bus and taxi companies running scheduled departures, throughout the day in some cases, to all major destinations.

PREVIOUS PAGES *A fuel and rest stop outside Kroonstad along the N1, South Africa's longest and busiest national road.*

ABOVE *This take-away food stop is in Touws River on the N1. The small railway town lies on the edge of the Great Karoo.*

Main national routes

Because South Africa's public transport system is limited, the most convenient and cost-effective way to travel is by car. Car rental is possible in all cities and major towns, fuel stations occur regularly on all major road networks and in towns, and there is no shortage of options for overnight stopovers. Because of South Africa's high rate of crime, it is advisable not to hitchhike and to avoid giving lifts to people you do not know. The following are some of the main national routes linking the major urban areas.

N1 – CAPE TOWN TO JOHANNESBURG AND BEYOND

For car lovers and self-drive enthusiasts, this route is the classic South African highway road trip. It has it all, from the stunning scenery through the mountain passes outside Cape Town across the vast open plains of the Karoo to the bustling and busy sections that lead into the gleaming metropolis of Johannesburg. Heading further north, the N1 continues through Pretoria and on to the northern border town of Musina. The N1 has toll gates from Bloemfontein to Musina.

The more popular option for this route passes through Colesberg and Bloemfontein, South Africa's legislative capital, but an alternative would be to branch off at Three Sisters and take the N12 via Kimberley and Klerksdorp. History buffs should consider a stopoff in Kimberley (www.kimberley-africa.com). It has the Big Hole – at one time the largest human-made hole in the world – and various museums associated with the diamond-mining industry and early settler history (www.museumsnc.co.za).

En route, the Lord Milner Hotel (www.matjiesfontein.com) in Matjiesfontein is a renowned stopover. This old Victorian hotel is the feature attraction of this tiny village that serves as a railway siding. As alternatives, the towns of Richmond and Colesberg (www.northerncape.org.za) have a variety of accommodation options.

Distances are as follows:
• Cape Town to Johannesburg: 1 402 km
• Johannesburg to Musina: 505 km
• Cape Town to Kimberley: 968 km
• Kimberley to Johannesburg: 476 km.

N2 – CAPE TOWN TO DURBAN

If the N1 is arguably the most scenic of the national highways, then the N2, no slouch for scenery either, is certainly the most varied and definitely the longest. For the most part, it follows the coastline between Cape Town and Durban, before heading up the North Coast and then inland to Ermelo in Mpumalanga.

Following this route alone could be a holiday in itself as it includes many regions that are wonderful destinations in their own right: the Garden Route (www.gardenroute.org.za), the Overberg (www.overberginfo.com) and both the South Coast (www.southcoast.kzn.org.za) and North Coast (www.dolphincoast.kzn.org.za) of KwaZulu-Natal. The route also passes through a number of cities, including Port Elizabeth, East London and Mthatha in the Eastern Cape.

Distances are as follows:
• Cape Town to George: 438 km
• George to Port Elizabeth: 335 km
• Port Elizabeth to Mthatha: 545 km
• Mthatha to Durban: 439 km.

N3 – JOHANNESBURG TO DURBAN

The N3, a toll road all the way, links Johannesburg and the greater Gauteng region to Durban, South Africa's third-largest city, principal port and popular holiday destination. It is an extremely busy route, with the highest concentration of heavy-duty truck traffic in South Africa.

For overnight options, stay in any of the delightful smaller towns off the N3 in the KwaZulu-Natal Midlands (www.zulu.org.za or www.kzn.org.za).

The distance is as follows:
• Johannesburg to Durban: 557 km.

N4 – JOHANNESBURG TO NELSPRUIT

With the coal-mining town of eMalahleni (formerly Witbank) and Maputo, the capital of Mozambique and a major port, on this route, it is another busy road. For holiday-makers, it's the easiest and quickest way to get to the Kruger National Park and the numerous tourist attractions spread across Mpumalanga. There is no need to dally though as it's only

the very last section of the road – from Waterval Boven to Nelspruit – that has any scenic appeal.

If overnighting is necessary, the small town of Belfast (Belfast Visitors Information Centre, Tel: +27 13 253-0408) can be tried, and for a stopover on the road to Mozambique, the town of Malalane (formerly Malelane) (www.malelane. co.za) is the best bet.

Going westwards via Rustenburg and Zeerust, the N4 is the major route into Botswana and its capital city, Gaborone.

Distances are as follows:

- Johannesburg to Nelspruit: 355 km
- Nelspruit to Maputo: 206 km
- Johannesburg to Lobatse (Botswana): 292 km.

N7 – CAPE TOWN TO NAMIBIA

The N7 is the major road heading into Namibia from the south, and is one of the more scenic and pleasant of the national routes. For the first few hours outside Cape Town the road passes through the Swartland, South Africa's primary wheat-growing region. Once it leaves Piketberg, the

ABOVE *Algoa Bay, with Port Elizabeth, South Africa's fifth-largest city, can be reached via the N2 between Cape Town and Durban.*
OPPOSITE *The N1 national road links Cape Town with Gauteng, and takes drivers through a variety of landscapes. This section is between Paarl and Worcester in the Western Cape.*

road enters the valleys, running adjacent to the Cederberg mountain range, which have some of the largest citrus and rooibos-tea farms in South Africa. From Vanrhynsdorp, the route enters Namaqualand and the harsher landscapes of the Nama Karoo biome. The last stretch – the mountainous regions beyond Springbok heading to the Orange River – is particularly appealing and best done between early August and early September, when the spectacular annual spring-flower bloom is at its most impressive (Flowerline, Tel: +27 83 910-1028).

En route, Clanwilliam (www.clanwilliam.info) is the most appealing stopover town, while, further north, Springbok (www.northerncape.org.za) has a wide selection of options, including the Goegap Nature Reserve just outside town.

ABOVE *The Roman Catholic Church at Pella, an old mission station a short distance off the N14.*

Distances are as follows:
- Cape Town to Springbok: 551 km
- Springbok to Namibian border: 118 km.

N14 – SPRINGBOK TO JOHANNESBURG

The N14 route is the quintessential long and lonely open-road option. The extended stretches of tar are bound by vast landscapes and endless horizons. The section between Springbok in the Northern Cape and Vryburg in North West province is the most appealing, so allocate your time for lingering accordingly. If there is time for diversions, the short drive off the N14 to Pella, a quaint old mission town that survives, oasis-like, in the harshness of the surrounding terrain, can be taken. Stopovers include Ebenaeser Guest House (www.augrabies-falls.com), a delightful country home set amongst vineyards just outside Kakamas, and, for those in search of an authentic throwback to the 1970s, the Pofadder Hotel in Pofadder, which will make for a humorous one-night stop (www.pofadderhotel.co.za).

Distances are as follows:
- Springbok to Upington: 378 km
- Upington to Johannesburg: 796 km.

Other options

TAKE A TRAIN

South Africa has two world-class train services that run between the major cities. The Blue Train (www.bluetrain.co.za) has been run by the national railway company for more than 50 years and has earned a reputation for its old-world luxury and elegance. It made its name carrying politicians and wealthy business folk on the Pretoria–Cape Town route, but now also operates between Pretoria and Durban, and can be hired for chartered rides as well.

Rovos Rail (www.rovos.co.za) started operating in 1989. It has come to be regarded as one of the world's premier operators of luxury train rides. It also covers the Pretoria–Cape Town route and does trips to various other capital cities and destinations in neighbouring countries.

CATCH A COACH OR BUS

Various coach and bus companies have overnight packages to all the major centres. Translux and City to City (www.translux.co.za), operated by the same holding company, are good options for the luxury and middle markets respectively. Backpackers are served by the famous Baz Bus (www.bazbus.com).

ABOVE *The Blue Train, renowned for its luxury and elegance, heads through the Cape Winelands region.*

CITY to CITY

PREVIOUS PAGES *Table Mountain forms a dramatic backdrop to the Koeberg Road site used by this street vendor in Cape Town.*

ABOVE *Early-morning fog blankets Cape Town's central business district and the areas surrounding the city centre.*

South Africa has a number of large cities that offer the very best of everything urban. They also embody the merging of European and African cultures and lifestyles that is the new South Africa. While Cape Town is rated by most international agencies and travel magazines as one of the world's best cities, each of the other cities too has its own appeal. Johannesburg is fast-paced and its size and energy alone are attractive features for some. The country's capital city, Pretoria, is a more stately option for those who need to be near the hub of the economy and the government, while the vibrant coastal city of Durban has its own distinctive character that reminds one of African coastal cities further north.

Cape Town

If you have limited time in South Africa and can plan only one destination, Cape Town has to be it. It is South Africa's oldest and most beautiful city. It is the third-largest metropolitan area, the legislative capital of the country, and where parliament sits – alternating with Pretoria – for six months of every year.

Often referred to as the Gateway to Africa, or more affectionately as the Mother City, it has an enormous amount to offer the visitor. It is certainly one of the world's most exciting recreational cities; you can experience everything that a cosmopolitan hub can offer as well as the great outdoors – all within the city limits (see the Travel South Africa chapter).

Beaches

Muizenberg and Bloubergstrand – The focus of these long, white beaches is pure action: kiteboarding, sea kayaking and surfing.

Clifton's beaches one to four – These are where the glamourous like to bronze themselves and be seen.

Camps Bay – This beach is the place to go for funky coffee shops, restaurants and nightlife.

Llandudno – At exclusive little coves like this the lucky locals reluctantly share their piece of heaven with the throngs of summer visitors.

Hout Bay and Kalk Bay – These original fishing communities, with their own harbours, have become sought-after urban areas and great places to visit.

Simon's Town – This quaint town steeped in naval history has an old English feel. It is also home to one of the world's few mainland-based colonies of penguins. You can view this endangered breeding colony, situated at Boulders beach, from close up. Please be very careful not to disturb these shy creatures. During the summer the beach boardwalks can be overcrowded with onlookers. Try to avoid the busiest times of the day.

Table Mountain

Table Mountain, managed by the South African National Parks (SANParks) (www.tmnp.co.za), is a dramatic focal point. It towers over the entire city, and is visible from every angle, near or far. The mountain is not only a powerful geological feature, but is also the source of many a mythical or imaginative historical story.

There are a number of access points to the mountain. The front of the table, made up of sheer cliffs, rises above the central city (known as the City Bowl). Rock climbers make use of these vertical faces, as does the Table Mountain Aerial Cableway, which is a breathtaking way of getting to the 1 086-m summit (www.tablemountain.net).

The more energetic head further along the contour road from the cable car's base station and find the start of the Platteklip Gorge access route. The flat-topped table is flanked by the smaller peaks of Devil's Peak on one side and Lion's Head and Signal Hill on the other. These are great to hike. Be aware, though, that these routes at times have been plagued by petty thieves. Hike in groups and don't carry unnecessary valuables.

Kirstenbosch National Botanical Garden

The immensely popular Kirstenbosch National Botanical Garden is the world's only botanical garden situated in a World Heritage Site. The site, known as the Cape Floral Region, gained its heritage status in 2004.

Perched on the slopes of Table Mountain, this remarkable national treasure provides gentle garden walks as well as steeper contour paths, and offers an access route to the summit of the mountain via the infamous Skeleton Gorge, only for the fit and able (www.sanbi.org).

Cape Point

Cape Point, the tip of the Cape Peninsula, in the Table Mountain National Park, has fantastic ocean views of the place where, some claim, the cold Atlantic and warm Indian oceans meet. More accurately, the meeting point is further south, at Cape Agulhas. Cape Point has a large variety of pelagic birds, several mammal species including zebra and eland, and small reptiles. Chacma baboons are in abundance here. Always fun to see, these beasts have become a nuisance due to visitors feeding them, which is strictly prohibited.

City centre

Colonial architecture – The city has some beautiful old British and Dutch colonial architecture, with the City Hall, Groote Kerk and Houses of Parliament being amongst a number worth seeing. The Cape of Good Hope Castle, built in the 1600s, marks the arrival of the first European settlers at the Cape.

CBD – The CBD is a combination of old and new. A perfect example of this is Greenmarket Square. The original cobbled plaza, surrounded by some beautiful old balconied buildings, is now home to a contemporary market filled with ethnic artwork sold by traders from all over Africa.

Long St and Loop St – The city centre's two main shopping streets are characterful, buzzing stretches of cafés, restaurants, nightclubs and colourful shops offering alternative label clothing and innovative wares. This area is a distinct mix of old, new, European and African.

V&A Waterfront

Shopping – For a mall experience that will rank with the best Europe and North America has to offer, head to the busy V&A Waterfront (www.waterfront.co.za). It also offers an array of coffee shops, restaurants and other entertainment options, and serves as the starting point for trips to Robben Island.

Two Oceans Aquarium – A highlight, the aquarium (www.aquarium.co.za) displays a vast selection of marine life. For an unusual experience, qualified divers can swim with ragged-tooth sharks, stingrays and other fun denizens of the deep.

Bo-Kaap

On the lower slopes of Signal Hill, the site of the historic noon gun, sits a colourful suburb largely inhabited by the Cape Malay community. Home to South Africa's first mosque, built in 1798, Bo-Kaap originally developed around the many slaves brought in from the East in the early days of the Cape Colony. The eye-catching Georgian-style terrace houses of the Bo-Kaap have been painted in a wonderful array of colours.

Robben Island

Made famous by its jail's most well-known inmate, Nelson Mandela, this World Heritage Site is a 'must see' excursion. Situated in the heart of Table Bay, the small, flat island is visible from almost every angle of the city. No longer a prison, it now operates as a monument to the fight for freedom, where ex-inmates guide you through the buildings as well as the history of the island. A remarkable demonstration of reconciliation, this symbol of the liberation struggle is a fascinating destination for any traveller to South Africa (www.robben-island.org.za).

Cape wine routes

South Africa has, without doubt, the most beautiful wine routes in the New World wine-producing areas. The best of South Africa's historic architecture is to be found on the old wine estates. Beautiful Dutch-gabled manor houses, dating back to the eighteenth century, form typical backdrops to many vineyards. Chosen for their splendid settings, many of these early estates are also established in the foothills of magnificent mountains. Up until quite recently, South Africa's wine routes were perhaps worth visiting for their beauty alone, but now the wine is also world class.

The Cape wine-producing areas are divided into 13 distinct regions, with the Constantia wine area being remarkable in that it is situated on the slopes of Table Mountain, in the

The Bo-Kaap in Cape Town is well known for its brightly painted homes and narrow streets.

TOP *Klein Constantia is one of nine recognised wine estates within the confines of the city of Cape Town.*

ABOVE *The historic Groot Constantia wine estate is as well known for its gracious manor house as it is for its wines.*

heart of Cape Town, and the Stellenbosch wine route being the most beautiful and prestigious. Although really good red wines and white wines are produced throughout the Cape, the Constantia and Walker Bay routes are known for white wines, and the Stellenbosch, Helderberg and Franschhoek routes for the reds.

Cape Point Vineyards, set apart and en route to Cape Point, is a fairly new concern, yet it has recently been voted South Africa's winery of the year. Don't miss out on tasting its award-winning Sauvignon Blanc.

Vergelegen, in the Somerset West area, is one of the most respected and historic estates, with a state-of-the-art cellar. Its flagship reds are unbeatable.

The farm Rustenberg, on the foothills of the Simonsberg, has continued centuries of excellence and produces world-class red wines in significant quantities. The South African National Heritage Council granted the estate 'natural and historical heritage status' in 2004. (Once granted heritage status, these sites are registered with the Department of Environmental Affairs and Tourism.) Rustenberg's Peter Barlow Cabernet Sauvignon and John X Merriman Bordeaux-style blend are some of South Africa's greatest ever examples of their type.

Many estates have fabulous restaurants on site. Constantia Uitsig in Cape Town, Haute Cabrière Cellar in Franschhoek, and Terroir, on the Kleine Zalze Estate in Stellenbosch, are a few of the many highly recommended options. For further information consult a copy of the invaluable *Platter's Wine Guide* (www.platteronline.com) or go to www.wineroute.co.za

The following websites cover accommodation, transport, restaurants, entertainment and other information: www.capetown.gopassport.com; www.rossouwsrestaurants.com; www.tourismcapetown.co.za; www.capetowninfo.co.za

Johannesburg and Soweto

Johannesburg is the largest and most populous city in South Africa, and while it has never been the capital, since the beginning of the twentieth century, it has been the principal city in terms of the economy. Also known as Jozi or Joburg to the locals, it is the provincial capital of Gauteng and the largest economic hub on the continent of Africa. Population-wise, the greater metropolis – which includes the West Rand, East Rand, Soweto and Sandton – consists of approximately eight million people. It is the third-largest metropolis in Africa, after Cairo in Egypt and Lagos in Nigeria.

The city has always been about opportunity, business and the pursuit of financial fortunes; it owes its very existence to the discovery of gold. The first strike took place back in 1886. Ever since then, the lure has been irresistible as people have come from South Africa's rural regions, from every corner of the African continent and from across the globe to stake their claims.

And for so many, the city has delivered. The gold discoveries gave rise to the Johannesburg Securities Exchange and, from the early 1900s, the major mining houses that would grow to play the most influential role in the development of the South African economy. All based in Johannesburg and controlled by individuals and families that became known as the Randlords, these mining companies are still the primary barometers of South Africa's economic health.

However, not all benefited as they should have, as Johannesburg and the mining industry also became the focus of South Africa's apartheid legislation. The migrant labour system, job discrimination and the hostel system all stemmed from the mining industry, and the gains of the wealthy white classes came at the expense of the hundreds of thousands of black labourers who toiled on the mines for a pittance.

Today, the city typifies everything that comes with a global metropolis: massive skyscrapers housing corporate headquarters, inner-city refurbishment projects and, in the suburbs, shopping malls, housing estates and satellite centres. All these are linked by a substantial network of

ABOVE *The old Johannesburg Securities Exchange building at the bottom end of Jozi's city centre.*

ABOVE *The iconic Nelson Mandela Bridge, with the Johannesburg city skyline in the background.*

crowded highways and byways that carry some of Africa's heaviest load of traffic. But Johannesburg also has an undeniably African feel, as the mix of developed and less developed world is there for all to see. Informal markets, sprawling townships and poverty-stricken squatter camps are found amidst the concrete, glass and manicured lawns.

Johannesburg has never been a big tourism attraction, partly because it can't compete with the likes of Cape Town or Durban and, more recently, because the horrific crime statistics have become a major deterrent. But since O.R. Tambo International airport — the largest and busiest airport in Africa — is the gateway to South Africa and a major link to so many other countries on the continent, most people landing there end up having to spend a few days in Johannesburg's vibrant embrace. If you find yourself with time in Johannesburg, here are a few options.

Apartheid Museum

Opened in 2001, this multidisciplinary museum covers the rise and fall of the apartheid era and the atrocities committed over that time (www.apartheidmuseum.org).

Johannesburg Art Gallery

An impressive collection of works spanning five centuries and covering artists, both early and contemporary, from Europe and Africa (www.joburg.org.za).

Old Fort and Constitutional Hill

This precinct focuses on South Africa's path to democracy. It includes the new Constitutional Court, built alongside the notorious Old Fort prison complex, which housed many of apartheid's opponents (www.constitutionhill.org.za).

Rosebank Rooftop Market

Held every Sunday on the rooftop parking of the Rosebank Mall, this market has everything and more.

Cradle of Humankind

Located outside Johannesburg, this World Heritage Site contains a number of important sites, which have yielded more than 950 hominid fossils, making this one of the richest concentrations in the world. Some of the finds are estimated to be between 3 and 3.5 million years old. The site also includes a number of complexes, including the Sterkfontein Caves and the Wonder Cave. For anyone with an interest in humankind's ancestral history, a visit to the Cradle of Humankind is a must (www.cradleofhumankind.co.za).

Gold mines

The Chamber of Mines organises extremely informative tours down working gold mines situated just outside Johannesburg (www.bullion.org.za).

Soweto

A visit to Soweto, the largest township in South Africa, is also a must (see The Life and Soul chapter). The leaders of apartheid established Soweto as a dumping ground for black people forcibly removed from urban areas and as a pool of cheap migrant workers. In the ultimate irony, this dumping ground became the hotbed of resistance that eventually led to the implosion of the then government. A township tour must include:

Hector Pieterson Museum – A powerful and compelling narrative of the Soweto Uprisings, which took place in 1976, and a commemoration of those who lost their lives. It is on the corner of Khumalo and Pela streets in Orlando West, Soweto (www.sowetouprisings.com).

Vilakazi Street – The is where two of South Africa's and Soweto's most famous residents, Nelson Mandela and Desmond Tutu, have homes.

Tavern time – A traditional tavern is a great way to mix with the locals; ask your guide to book lunch at one of the many vibey taverns around the township.

The following websites cover accommodation, restaurants, entertainment and other tourist information: www.gauteng.net; www.joburgtourism.com; www.joburg.org.za. For more information on Soweto, go to: www.sowetotourism.com; www.sowetotourism.co.za

ABOVE *These power-station cooling towers are a famous landmark in Soweto.*

91

Pretoria

Once the bastion of the apartheid government and every-thing Afrikaner, the city has over the last decade become a cosmopolitan metropolis representative of the new South Africa. This transformation is reflected in moves by the ANC-led city council to have the name changed to Tshwane, the name of the son of an African chief who ruled in the area during the 1700s. If the name change goes ahead, Pretoria, named after the Boer leader Andries Pretorius, would still survive, but only as a small precinct in the city centre.

In the meantime, the greater region has had an official name change. If one takes into account the surrounding residential areas of Centurion, Atteridgeville, Mabopane,

Soshanguve and Mamelodi, then the City of Tshwane Metropolitan Municipality has a population in excess of 2.5 million. And such has been the extent of urban development between Tshwane and Johannesburg to the south that the two centres are likely to merge into one massive metropolitan area within the next decade.

Often also referred to as the Jacaranda City because of the purple-blossomed exotic trees that line many of its

avenues and streets, this city serves as the executive or administrative seat of government and is the official capital of the country. The city is also well known for its numerous landmark buildings: the impressive Union Buildings, designed by Sir Herbert Baker; the University of South Africa (UNISA) campus; the Voortrekker Monument and its remarkable roof design; the South African Council for Scientific and Industrial Research (CSIR); and the State Theatre, in the city centre. Depending on the length of your stay, try to see some of the sights listed below.

Museums
Transvaal Museum – Numerous natural history displays, including rare fossil finds from Sterkfontein, the Cradle of Humankind, are displayed here.
Other museums – These include the Smuts Museum, Kruger House, the National Cultural History Museum and the Sammy Marks Museum.

Union Buildings
Overlooking Pretoria, these buildings are the official seat of government and house the offices of the President. If you have time for only one excursion, then make sure you visit this one.

Voortrekker Monument
Situated on Monument Hill, this massive structure was built to honour the Boer pioneers (the Voortrekkers) who left the Cape Colony in the mid-1800s (www.voortrekkermon.org.za).

National Botanical Gardens
These offer sanity in the city centre. Check out the local press for evening music concerts in the gardens.

The following websites cover accommodation, restaurants, entertainment and other information: www.pretoria.co.za; www.ptaweb.co.za; www.tshwane.gov.za

LEFT *Designed by Sir Herbert Baker, the Union Buildings in Pretoria are the headquarters of South Africa's civil service and government administration.*

surf and the great outdoors. The beaches are also why the city has such a great reputation amongst the global surfing set as a treasured hang-out. The feature attraction is the Golden Mile, which forms the city's beachfront, stretching from South Beach to the Suncoast Casino on the north side. With a wide-paved promenade separating the ocean from rows of plush multistorey hotels, Art Deco apartment blocks, countless fast-food outlets and gaudy amusement parks, it's a delightfully vibrant and energetic place to be, no matter what time of day. And one row back, the main beachfront road is always bustling with hawkers, pedestrians, voyeurs and the ever-present Zulu rickshaw operators, ready to pull you around town in their colourful carts.

The city centre lies a few blocks back, and beyond the north—south highway link, the residential areas begin as the Berea Ridge gathers height. The coastal towns of Umhlanga and Ballito on the North Coast and Amanzimtoti on the South Coast are very much regarded as part of the Durban scene.

Of all South Africa's cities, Durban can lay claim to being the most cosmopolitan. It lies in the middle of the ancient Zulu kingdom, has a strong British settler community, and because contract labourers were brought from India in the late 1800s to work the sugar-cane fields, it has one of the largest Indian populations living outside India. This mix is at the core of the palpably multicultural atmosphere that permeates all aspects of life in the city.

The Golden Mile

Whether it's for the sea and sun, a midday or evening meal or merely a casual stroll, this is a great place to soak up the cosmopolitan atmosphere of the city.

uShaka Marine World

This glitzy entertainment centre has loads of shops and restaurants. The highlight is the marvellous aquarium with numerous marine exhibits (www.ushakamarineworld.co.za).

ABOVE LEFT *Rickshaw operators, wearing flamboyant headdresses, are a common sight on the Golden Mile along Durban's beachfront.*
OPPOSITE *Of all the cities in South Africa, Durban can claim to be the most cosmopolitan.*

Durban

Situated on the eastern coast of South Africa, this subtropical city is South Africa's third largest and, after Cape Town, the second most popular city destination for tourists. Durban is also the economic hub of the greater eThekwini Metro, which includes the surrounding municipalities and the townships of KwaMashu and Umlazi. It is South Africa's most important container port and one of the 10 busiest ports worldwide.

Because of its balmy climate and endless golden beaches, lapped by the warm waters of the Indian Ocean, Durban is really all about having loads of fun in the sea and

Natal Sharks Board

Situated in Umhlanga, north of Durban, this research and educational centre will open the amazing world of sharks to you (www.shark.co.za). For the more adventurous, boat trips off the coast of Durban can also be arranged.

A curry dinner

Durban has the best authentic Indian restaurants, so treat yourself to a curry in one of the many around town.

Durban Art Gallery

This gallery is the city's most comprehensive, with everything from local art and artefacts to English masterpieces.

Victoria Street Market

Although somewhat in the back streets, Durban's original Indian market offers a variety of crafts, spices, fruit, antiques and other items.

Township tour

Operators offer tours into the townships surrounding Durban (www.kzn.org.za).

Further afield: Pietermaritzburg

Pietermaritzburg, the provincial capital of KwaZulu-Natal, lies 70 km along the N3 from Durban towards Johannesburg. Although transformed into a modern African city, it still has something of an old colonial feel to it and is worth a visit for those particularly interested in South Africa's history (www. pmbtourism.co.za).

Other attractions include the KwaZulu-Natal National Botanical Garden and the Butterflies for Africa complex (www. butterflies.co.za), which boasts a walk-through butterfly house that contains both exotic and indigenous butterflies.

The following websites cover accommodation, restaurants, entertainment and other information: www.durban.co.za; www.durban-direct.com; www.durbanexperience.co.za

LEFT *A mime artist holds his pose along Durban's beachfront, which is an exciting mix of grand hotels, restaurants and bars, amusement parks and curio stalls.*

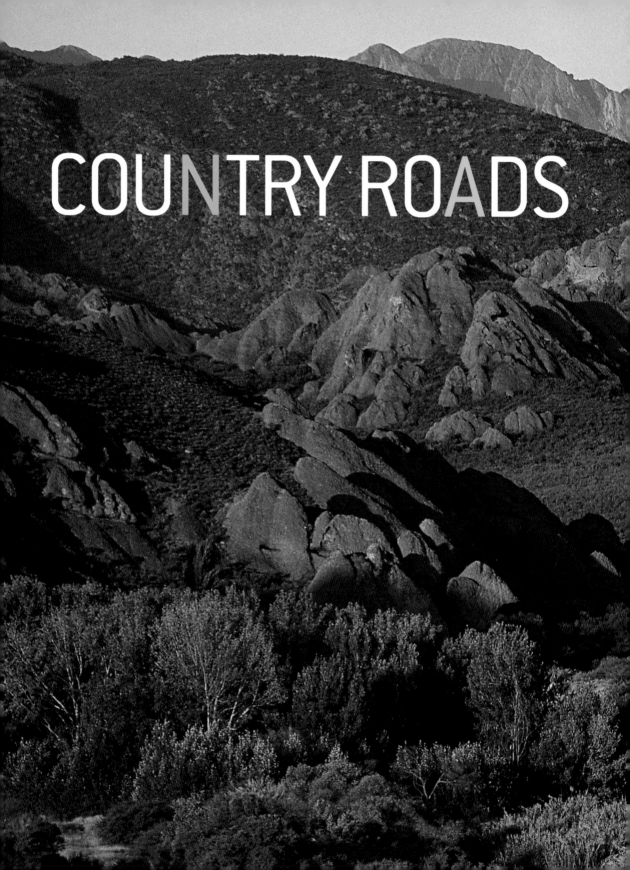

COUNTRY ROADS

PREVIOUS PAGES *The sandstone hills of Red Mountain outside Calitzdorp in the Western Cape.*

ABOVE *Brightly coloured fishing boats along the beach at Paternoster on the West Coast.*

For those who enjoy the thrill of heading out with an open mind and a map, this is your chance to explore the road less travelled – from the vast expanses of both the Great and Little Karoo through the more popular Garden Route and Overberg to the little-known Kalahari and beyond. The countless back roads and country lanes will take you to towns and villages brimming with charm, character and delightfully welcoming folk. These roads are best done by car, but before heading out check road conditions with the nearest tourist information centre. There are also bus and train services that will get you to many of the destinations.

Little Karoo

Heading along the N1 highway from Cape Town, you will encounter the Huguenot Tunnel and, emerging on the other side, will find yourself in an environment entirely different from Cape Town and its surrounds. Take the country road to Worcester and your journey into some of South Africa's most delightful rural life has begun.

BREEDE RIVER WINELANDS

The road from Cape Town to the Little Karoo takes you through the Breede River winelands, which includes the towns of Worcester, Robertson, Ashton, Montagu, McGregor and Bonnievale. Two great wine-related events are hosted by this valley: the Wacky Wine Weekend, held over the first

ABOVE *The Karoo town of De Rust with the Swartberg mountains in the background.*

weekend of June (www.wackywineweekend.com), and the popular Wine on the River Festival, held in October (www.wineonriver.com).

The area has a plethora of great guesthouses and self-catering accommodation options, many of which are on the wine estates. Free tastings of wine are available on most farms. Although this is a fertile and productive valley, it is markedly drier than Cape Town and hints at the more arid landscapes that become the Little Karoo – or the *Klein Karoo* as it is known in Afrikaans – just a short drive further east.

ROUTE 62

The charming Route 62 starts at Montagu and winds its way eastwards through the Little Karoo. Flanked on either side by stark mountain ranges, it takes you into the very heart of South Africa's country culture. The towns – or *dorpe* as they are called in Afrikaans – are often centred on an old church, whose steeple can be seen piercing the cloudless blue sky from miles away. Life is slow and peaceful here, with the characteristic architecture of large, square, thick-walled homes surrounded by verandahs for protection from the midday sun. Many are a mix of Victorian and Cape Dutch features. Smallholdings are often found in the centre of these towns, with windmills in their gardens. Sheep and goats and *leiwater* (irrigation water) furrows are features of many of the towns in the Little Karoo.

Little Karoo Wine Route

The Little Karoo Wine Route is one of the main attractions of a Route 62 road trip. It begins in Montagu – well known for its *soeters* (dessert wines) – and includes Barrydale (famous for the pot still brandy produced here) and Calitzdorp (home to South Africa's award-winning port wine) before ending in De Rust. This very pretty hamlet is a great contributor to the annual wine and food festival that takes place along the route in December (www.sa-venues.com; www.kleinkaroowines.co.za). For accommodation here, the House Martin is a lovely lodge (www.housemartin.co.za), or try Oulap, an old country house 15 km east of town (Tel: +27 44 241-2250). The award-winnng Boplaas Cellar in Calitzdorp is definitely worth a visit (www.boplaas.co.za), as is the De Krans Cellar (Tel: +27 44 213-3314) on the outskirts of the town.

Barrydale and Ladismith

Some of these Little Karoo towns have, in recent years, been given a boost of fresh energy and a trendy edge by the increasing numbers of young and creative folk settling here.

Barrydale – This town has a number of lovely renovated guesthouses, hotels and coffee shops that are definitely worthy of an overnight stop.

Ladismith – This town lies in the shadow of the Towerkop Mountain peak. On the outskirts are some wonderful old farmhouses that have been converted into guesthouses. They are particularly renowned for their delicious traditional Afrikaner cooking (www.sa-venues.com).

Oudtshoorn and surrounds

Ostriches – Known as the ostrich capital of the Klein Karoo, Oudtshoorn has some splendid architectural icons, referred to as *volstruispaleise* ('ostrich palaces' in Afrikaans). These mansions are reminders of the ostrich feather boom of the early 1900s, when local farmers made fortunes overnight. Today the ostriches are farmed for meat, eggs and feathers.

Klein Karoo Nasionale Kunstefees – Oudtshoorn is the host of this annual arts festival (Little Karoo National Arts Festival), held every year in autumn (www.oudtshoorninfo.com).

Gamkaberg Nature Reserve – Southeast of Oudtshoorn is this wonderful wilderness area, managed by CapeNature. It has a number of great accommodation options, ranging from rustic bush lodges to camping (www.capenature.org.za).

Township tour – The character of many small towns has changed significantly since the end of apartheid. Previously dominated by the Afrikaans farming community and coloured labourers who lived on the farms, the towns now have burgeoning black townships that accommodate the influx of Xhosa people who come in search of work. A worthwhile excursion in Oudtshoorn is a township tour led by an innovative local entrepreneur (Thando's Township Tours, Tel: +27 72 321-7947; e-mail: thando@tsamail.co.za).

Spectacular passes and caves – Because this Little Karoo area is sandwiched between parallel mountain ranges – the Langeberg and Outeniqua mountains in the south and Groot Swartberge in the north – it may be accessed via a number of spectacular passes. If back-country journeys are your thing, an absolute highlight would be a route through the Little

TOP *The Dutch Reformed Church in Calitzdorp.*
LEFT *The homely dining room of the Willow Historical Guest House in Willowmore.*
ABOVE *An antique store in De Rust.*

103

ABOVE *A section of the spectacular Swartberg Pass, which links Oudtshoorn with the Karoo town of Prince Albert.*

Karoo that would take you off the R62 onto the R327. Head to the tiny hamlet of Van Wyksdorp, where you will find the turnoff for the Rooiberg Pass. This dramatic landscape can be even better explored if you choose to overnight in the Red Mountain Nature Reserve (www.debergkant.co.za). North of Oudtshoorn you will encounter the Cango Caves tucked away in the foothills of the Swartberg mountains. These limestone caverns, more than 20 million years old, are one of South Africa's great natural wonders (www.cangocaves.co.za). From here head to the charming village of Prince Albert over the undulating red rock formations of the Swartberg Pass. Opened in 1888, this untarred road, winding to the summit at 1 583 m, is an extraordinary engineering feat in itself.

Prince Albert – A number of memorable lodges and B&Bs here will enhance your visit. A favoured old homestead, De Bergkant Lodge, is a great recommendation (www.debergkant.co.za). From Prince Albert head to the village of Klaarstroom and on through yet another dramatic pass, Meiringspoort, to De Rust.

Gamkaskloof – A most unusual detour from the Swartberg Pass but suitable for 4x4s only takes you down into a hidden valley, known to the locals as Die Hel. This fascinating place was home to a small, proud community who lived here in isolation for more than 100 years. Access was by foot or horseback until a steep and windy road was finally carved down into the valley in 1962. A number of the old homes have been renovated by members of the original families and others by CapeNature. These are all available for rent (www.patourism.co.za; www.capenature.org.za).

WILLOWMORE

This favourite village lies somewhere between the Great Karoo, the Little Karoo and the Baviaanskloof in the Eastern Cape. Make a stop at the Willow Historical Guest House (www.willowguesthouse.co.za). This beautiful Victorian home and adjacent cottages will afford you the best opportunity to experience old-style country hospitality.

FRUIT-GROWING REGIONS

Another worthwhile option is to head westwards from Montagu, at the start of R62, and into the fruit-growing regions of Wellington, Ceres, Wolseley and Tulbagh. These towns are

all linked by winding country roads that cover some very scenic terrain, including various mountain passes. Tulbagh has the added attraction of being an historic town with some wonderful museums and many examples of homes built in the traditional Cape Dutch architecture. The Tulbagh Country Manor Guest House (www.tulbaghguesthouse.co.za), a national monument, is one of the most authentic examples and a charming place to stay.

Great Karoo

These arid lands are characterised by big skies with endless horizons, and by blazing summers and icy winters. Few visitors to the communities, farms and towns on this semidesert plateau remain untouched by the magnificent scenery, history and tranquillity.

Humans have lived on this harsh land for more than 500 000 years. The Khoikhoi and San people, who left

ABOVE *Kranskop Peak, the highest in the Sneeuberg, outside Nieu-Bethesda in the Eastern Cape.*

their legacy in the form of rock art, gave the Karoo its name: *Karusa*, meaning 'dry', 'barren' or 'thirstland'. The Karoo is integral to the world of scientists, botanists, archaeologists, geologists and palaeontologists. It is an ancient, fossil-rich land and has the largest variety of succulents found anywhere on earth. Game – like springbok, klipspringer, kudu, eland and many other antelope species to which these plains and mountains are home – add to the interest of this area.

KAROO NATIONAL PARK

This park, on the outskirts of Beaufort West, provides a protected environment for antelope along with endangered black rhino, riverine rabbit, bat-eared fox, wild ostrich, lynx and Hartmann's mountain zebra. Lovely self-catering cottages and camping facilities are available within the park (www.sanparks.org).

GRAAFF-REINET AND SURROUNDS

Known as the Gem of the Karoo, this is the fourth-oldest town in South Africa (1786). Much of the old town has been preserved, and there are a number of heritage sites and museums worth a visit (www.graaffreinet.co.za). The Graaff-Reinet Information Centre offers a wealth of information (Tel: +27 49 892-5774 or +27 49 892-4248). In the heart of the town is the beautifully restored historic home of the *landdrost* (chief magistrate), built in 1804, and now the site of the Drostdy Hotel (Tel: +27 49 892-2161; www.drostdy. co.za). It is a great place to stay if you want to experience the best the town has to offer.

Sheep farms

To get a real feel of life in the Great Karoo, a stay on one of the surrounding sheep farms offering authentic and gracious hospitality is highly recommended. Some 50 km south of Graaff-Reinet lies the beautiful and historic farm Wheatlands (Tel: +27 49 891-0422/4; www.wheatlands.co.za), and 27 km north of Graaff-Reinet is the Bloemhof homestead.

ABOVE *Donkey carts are still the most regularly used form of transport by farm labourers of the Little Karoo and Great Karoo.*

This grand old house is presently occupied by its seventh generation of the Murray family (Tel: +27 49 892-3234 or +27 49 840-0203; e-mail: murraybloemhof@yebo.co.za).

Camdeboo National Park

Graaff-Reinet is almost entirely surrounded by one of South Africa's newest national parks, Camdeboo National Park. Proclaimed in 2005, the park protects a diverse spectrum of wildlife, but the premier attraction of the park is the Valley of Desolation. This extraordinary natural wonder, with its magnificent dolerite pillars rising to heights of 120 m, was first declared a National Monument in 1939 (www.sanparks.org).

NIEU-BETHESDA

This quaint town was founded in 1878 by farmers tired of having to travel to Graaff-Reinet to attend church on Sundays. The farmers eventually decided to establish their own

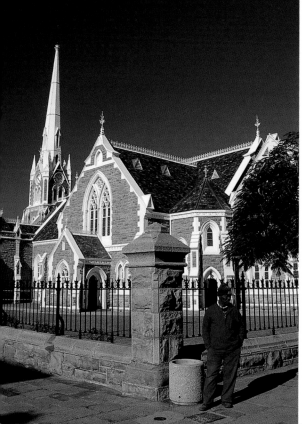

Matjiesfontein and Sutherland

Begin this journey in the historic village of Matjiesfontein, just off the N1 highway, and head north to Sutherland. While this village has an old-fashioned character, it does have a very modern feature: the sophisticated Southern African Large Telescope (SALT), which can be visited for an unforgettable stargazing experience (www.saao.ac.za; Tel: +27 23 571-1265). From here, hit the dirt roads to Fraserburg and on to Loxton. There are two circular route options from here.

Loxton to Victoria West – The first option is to swing east from Loxton and head for Victoria West, another charming farming town. The De Oude Scholen B&B (Tel: +27 73 607-2938) is a great stopover here.

Loxton to Calvinia – Alternatively, from Loxton, head to Carnarvon and then west into the Hantamsberg and the town, Calvinia. The main attraction here is Die Hantam Huis, an old, authentic Cape Dutch homestead which houses the very best restaurant in the whole Karoo (www.calvinia. co.za; e-mail: hantamhuis@calvinia.co.za).

ABOVE *The Dutch Reformed Church in Graaff-Reinet is one of many architectural delights the town has to offer.*

Dutch Reformed Church parish. This tiny and extremely picturesque hamlet, only 50 km north of Graaff-Reinet, was made famous in the mid-1980s by Athol Fugard, the internationally renowned South African playwright. His work *The Road to Mecca* was based on a town local, Helen Martins, and her extraordinary home, The Owl House, which remains one of the town's most important attractions. Today there are a number of fabulous little shops, art galleries, restaurants and places to stay. For more information contact Idil Sheard (Tel: +27 49 841-1635).

QUIETER TOWNS

There is a lovely route that will allow you to experience the northern and western sections of the barren Karoo landscape. It is a quieter, starker and lonelier drive and fewer changes have been made over time to the little towns along this route.

ABOVE *A craft-seller's roadside stall outside the Great Karoo town of Cradock in the Eastern Cape.*

Overberg

In so many ways the Overberg (www.overberg.co.za) region resembles a mini-Karoo. The scenery, the tranquillity, the country towns and the amiable farming-folk – they're all here, but they come with a more agreeable climate and some spectacular coastlines. The Overberg covers the very southern extremes of the Western Cape between the Hottentots Holland mountains, which form the western boundary of the Overberg, and Swellendam, the regions easternmost boundary. It includes the second most important wheat-growing district, one of the largest fruit-growing valleys, the southernmost tip of Africa, the breeding stronghold of the Blue Crane, some of the world's best opportunities for whale-watching, and the Kogelberg Biosphere Reserve.

HERMANUS

Situated 120 km from Cape Town, the seaside town of Hermanus (www.hermanus.co.za/info) was once a small and rustic fishing village, but because of its whale-watching opportunities, it has now become one of South Africa's favourite holiday resorts. It is the country's premier whale-watching destination and from July to late November, the shores of the town offer spectacular sightings of southern right and humpback whales. Other options for viewing the whales include boat cruises and kayak tours that depart from the local harbour. The World Wide Fund for Nature (WWF) has rated Hermanus as one of the 12 best whale-viewing sites in the world.

ABOVE *Hermanus, on the southern Cape coast, is one of South Africa's most popular coastal destinations.*

SWELLENDAM

Lying at the foothills of the Langeberg mountains, Swellendam (www.swellendamtourism.co.za), is the third oldest town in South Africa. With its broad main road, tree-lined streets and old historic buildings and museums, it's a town well worth a stopover.

OTHER OVERBERG TOWNS

Other towns to visit in the Overberg include the following:

L'Agulhas – This town is at Cape Agulhas, the southernmost tip of Africa and where the Indian and Atlantic oceans meet.

Caledon, Napier and Bredasdorp – These three wheat-farming towns have their own unique charm.

Hemel en Aarde Valley – Nestled between Caledon and Hermanus, this picturesque country district is well known for its award-winning wine estates.

Gansbaai – The shark-cage diving industry is based here.

Arniston – An historic fishing village, Arniston has some wonderfully remote beaches. It is close to two nature reserves – the De Hoop and De Mond nature reserves.

Elim – The tiny Moravian hamlet of Elim was founded in 1824. It is situated along the back roads between Bredasdorp and Gansbaai, and is a delightful diversion.

ABOVE *A family from the village of Suurbraak in the Western Cape.*
BELOW *Wheat fields in the Overberg, the second largest wheat-producing region in South Africa.*

Garden Route

The stretch of coastline that runs between Mossel Bay and Port Elizabeth, known as the Garden Route, has long been considered one of the greatest attractions of South Africa. While in recent years unchecked development and suburban sprawl have changed the nature of the small towns that dot the coastline and scarred some of the natural environment, the Garden Route nevertheless still has some inspiring attractions, including sweeping bays, long stretches of white, sandy beaches, warm surf, lagoons, lakes, forests and coastal mountains.

MOSSEL BAY

This town in the west has some fine beaches and an excellent golf course.

GEORGE

George has a number of golf courses regarded as world class. Nestled at the foothills of some rather imposing peaks, this inland town is home to Fancourt, one of South Africa's most prestigious golf estates and hotels (www.fancourt.co.za).

VICTORIA BAY

The George locals consider Victoria Bay their beach spot. This cosy and pretty little cove just 20 minutes from George provides safe swimming and a wonderful point break for the avid surfer. There is only one strip of little houses along the bay, and a campsite. Many of these houses are available for rent. The highlight though is the delightful Land's End B&B at the very end of the single road, overlooking the surf spot (www.vicbay.com).

WILDERNESS

Wilderness is flanked by miles of wild beach and a tranquil lagoon linked to an inland lake system that provides great opportunities for water sports and birding.

SEDGEFIELD

Sedgefield's natural beauty is hidden from the passer-by. Head towards the sea from the national highway and find this unexpected gem of a coastal community perched on the edge of the Swartvlei lagoon.

BUFFALO BAY

This seaside town is known as much for its unusual mix of seaside homes – certainly not glamorous or grand, but definitely representative of an element of South African culture – as for its wonderful bay. At low tide, the beach can be walked or mountain biked all the way to neighbouring Brenton-on-Sea.

KNYSNA

Knysna is a multifaceted and lively town with a number of attractions and festivals.

Staying on the Knysna lagoon – Knysna has a range of accommodation options: from tranquil island settings on the old, established Leisure Isle or the newly developed Thesen Islands to places with wonderful views over the water from the hills behind the town or from the well-known Knysna Heads. A great recommendation is Leisure Isle's sea-facing B&Bs, which can offer exclusive and private usage of this intimate island suburb (www.exploreafrica.co.za/wcape/groute). Another is the Phantom Forest Lodge, perched high up above the Knysna lagoon in beautiful indigenous forest (www.phantomforest.com).

Festivals – Knysna is the festival town on the Garden Route, with the fabulously gay Pink Loerie Mardi Gras held in May, the highly popular Oyster Festival in July and the Gastronomica Festival in September (www.tourismknysna.co.za).

PLETTENBERG BAY

Plettenberg Bay (known widely as 'Plett') has to be the *pièce de résistance* of the Garden Route, with its spectacular bay and beaches. The town – one of South Africa's most glamorous holiday destinations – is also where the country's elite flock to their beach houses over the busy Christmas season. Avoid this December rush and you will have a wonderful stay here as there is something for everyone: good restaurants, fine shopping, wonderful beaches and safe swimming.

ABOVE *A fisherman bides his time on the Knysna lagoon.*
LEFT *The beach at St Francis Bay in the Eastern Cape.*
BELOW *Pansy shells can be found along the many beaches of the Garden Route.*

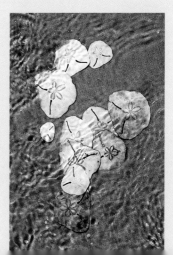

Robberg Nature Reserve – This peninsula makes up the southern arm of Plettenberg Bay. Hike the wild side to experience this windswept wilderness or make it to the end where you will feel as though you are standing at the tip of the world (www.capenature.org.za).

Dolphin and whale viewing – These activities are available during the winter months (www.oceanblueadventures.co.za). Viewing options include motorised launches, kayaking trips or vantage points on land.

Staying at the beach – Hire a house on the beach (www.rea.co.za) or stay in one of the superb guesthouses or lodges in the area. Hunter Hotels, which offer Tsala Treetop Lodge or the Hunter's Country House (a Relais & Châteaux establishment) are two of the very best (www.hunterhotels.com). A favoured beach choice is the Southern Cross Beach House B&B (www.southerncrossbeach.co.za), a lovely family-run affair. Innovative options, offering tranquil views of indigenous forest, are Hog Hollow (www.hog-hollow.com), and Trogon House and Forest Spa (www.trogonhouse.co.za).

NATURE'S VALLEY

In contrast to the sophistication of Plett is the understated village of nearby Nature's Valley. Nestled in lovely coastal

ABOVE The Afromontane forests along the Garden Route, particularly around Knysna and Nature's Valley, offer great hiking and birding opportunities.

montane forest, with only one very basic convenience store and restaurant, Nature's Valley's attraction is a long, beautiful beach and the surrounding Tsitsikamma Forest. It is where South Africa's most well-known hike, the Otter Trail, comes to an end (see the Travel South Africa chapter).

TSITSIKAMMA NATIONAL PARK

A forest and marine protected area, the Tsitsikamma National Park (www.sanparks.org) extends from Nature's Valley westwards for 80 km to the mouth of the Groot River.

CAPE ST FRANCIS

This town and the surrounding coastal villages offer further opportunities to experience the splendour of South Africa's long, white beaches and good surf.

JEFFREYS BAY

Jeffreys Bay is famous for its waves. It's a must for the international wave-rider (www.jeffreysbay.org).

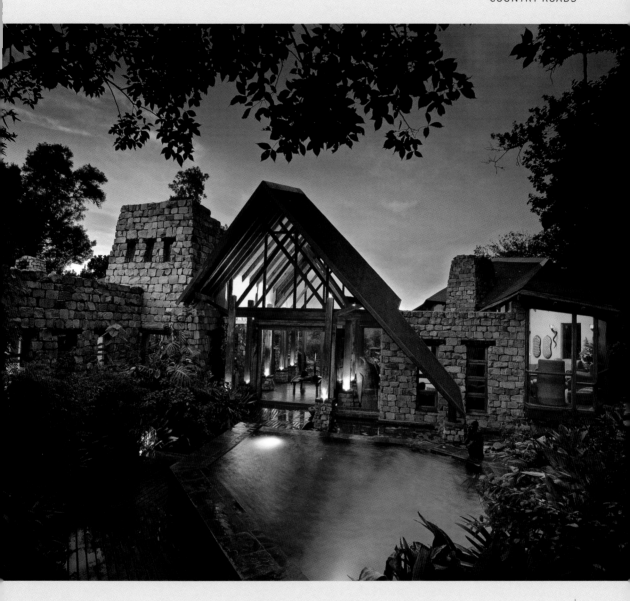

Tsala Treetop Lodge is one of the Garden Route's most sought-after stopovers.

Mpumalanga

Mpumalanga, with its dynamic capital, Nelspruit, is one of the fastest growing regions in South Africa. While manufacturing, agriculture, forestry and coal mining are all substantial contributors to the local economy, tourism has become the most significant. The province's main attractions are the Kruger National Park and the surrounding private game reserves (see the On Safari chapter).

TOURISM ROUTES

The province has seven designated tourism routes (www. mpumalanga.com), four of which are worth exploring.

The Highlands Meander

This route covers the central highland plateau and towns such as Mashishing, Dullstroom, Belfast and Machadodorp. **Waterval Boven** — This mountainous region offers great hiking trails and climbing for hard-core rock climbers. It is regarded as one of the best climbing destinations in Africa. **Belfast and Mashishing** — The upland rolling hill country between Belfast and Mashishing is one of the foremost trout-fishing destinations in South Africa.

ABOVE *Pineapples are commonly for sale along the roadside outside the town of Nelspruit in Mpumalanga.*

Long Tom Pass — For a scenic country drive, the magnificent R540 over the escarpment via the Long Tom Pass is a great alternative route into the Lowveld.

The Panorama

This route covers the central and northern escarpment. **Blyde River Canyon** — This spectacular feature is the most popular attraction. **Bourke's Luck Potholes** — This series of geological formations along the Motlatse River is fascinating. **God's Window** — Another appealing stopoff along the escarpment is this magnificent viewpoint. **Pilgrim's Rest and Sabie** — The old gold-rush town of Pilgrim's Rest and the forestry town of Sabie are interesting towns worth a visit.

The Cultural Heartland

This route covers the northwestern sector of Mpumalanga, along the Gauteng border. Tourism here is focused on the vibrant and colourful cultural exhibitions of the Ndebele people. Botshabelo and Loopspruit are the two most well-known cultural villages.

The Wild Frontier

This route extends down into the eastern Lowveld and includes the southern part of the Kruger National Park. **Barberton** — Set against the Bulembu mountains, this is another historic gold-rush town that is worth exploring for a day or two. The Royal Sheba Guesthouse (Tel: + 27 13 712-4564) is the recommended B&B in town. **Jane Goodall Institute Chimpanzee Sanctuary** — En route to Barberton from Nelspruit, be sure to stop off here (www. janegoodall.co.za).

BIRD-WATCHING

For birders, the southern grasslands of the Wakkerstroom district (Tourism Office, Tel: +27 17 730-0606) are a must. Nine of South Africa's endemic species are found here, and it is the best place for encountering Rudd's Lark and Botha's Lark. For accommodation, head to the charming Wetlands Country House & Sheds on the edge of town (www. wetlandscountryhouse.co.za).

The dramatic Blyde River Canyon in Mpumalanga.

Eastern Free State

Tucked beneath the foothills of the Maloti mountains on the border with Lesotho, the eastern Free State is a special corner of South Africa. The sandstone cliffs form a dramatic background to valleys of fertile crops and fields of cosmos, sunflowers and fruit trees. This is home to the peaceful Basotho people, who are distinctly recognisable when decked out in traditional garb.

A unique feature of the old towns and their rural architecture is the colonial buildings crafted from hand-hewn blocks taken from the sandstone cliffs (www.malotiroute.co.za).

CLARENS

The jewel of the region, Clarens is a prime outdoor recreation destination. The mountains offer great walks, birding, fly-fishing, horse riding and mountain biking. The town is also a haven for artists and, with more than a dozen art galleries, it is a great place to browse or find the perfect piece. The town has many good accommodation options (www.goclarens. co.za), most notably Lilliput House (www.infoclarens.com).

GOLDEN GATE HIGHLANDS NATIONAL PARK

The feature attraction of the area is Golden Gate Highlands National Park. The name is derived from the imposing 'Brandwag' rock, which stands vigil over this route to the Maloti mountains, glowing gold from the rays of the sun on its sandstone form. This truly beautiful park is a hiker's haven, where visitors can glimpse black wildebeest, eland, blesbok, zebra, oribi and springbok. Birders should make the effort to get here as there are a number of local specials, most significantly the Bearded Vulture. For overnight options, the accommodation ranges from rustic rest camps with tenting and caravan options to cabins, farmhouses and a hotel (www.sanparks.org).

FICKSBURG

Further south, the town of Ficksburg is known as the 'Cherry Capital' of South Africa. The farming community offers particular fun during the Cherry Festival, which takes place in November every year (www.ficksburg.org.za).

ABOVE *A country scene in the Clarens district, a rich agricultural area in the highlands of the eastern Free State.*

OPPOSITE *An old gravesite with the sandstone cliffs of Golden Gate Highlands National Park in the background.*

Kalahari

This is the place to be for those in search of wide open spaces and long and lonely roads. The greater region stretches west of the N12 across the harsh, dry landscapes of Namaqualand, and from north of the Cederberg mountains and Nuweveldberge to South Africa's border with Namibia and Botswana.

Solitude, silence and stark beauty – these are the characteristics that make the Kalahari such an immensely appealing place in which to travel. And then there are the small, dusty country towns, sun-drenched and filled with charm and character, that await you at the end of each stretch of road.

The region forms part of the Kalahari Basin, which is covered by a sand mantle that is the largest unbroken mass of sand that exists on the planet. While often referred to as the Kalahari Desert, it is in fact not a true desert, but rather an extended region of similar soil types characterised by their well-leached and nutrient-poor condition. The vegetation type is mostly scrub and acacia-type woodland, although these are interspersed with the characteristic rolling red dunes, which are often topped with blankets of faded yellow grass. The region experiences low and erratic rainfall and remarkable extremes of temperature.

While the Kgalagadi Transfrontier Park (see the On Safari chapter) is the region's most well-known destination, there are many other appealing sights and stopovers.

ABOVE *An elderly couple from the village of Pella in the Northern Cape.*
OPPOSITE *Good-quality dust roads make for convenient travelling through much of South Africa's countryside.*

THE RAPTOR ROUTE

For avid bird-watchers, the region offers wonderful raptor-viewing, particularly during the hotter summer months. More than 40 raptor and vulture species (South Africa has 67 listed species) and seven owl species (12 listed species) have been recorded. The route includes the triangle shaped by the Augrabies Falls National Park, the Tswalu Kalahari Reserve and the Kgalagadi Transfrontier Park.

AUGRABIES FALLS NATIONAL PARK

Augrabies Falls, the sixth largest waterfall in the world, lies west of Upington. Where the ancient granite rocks edging the Orange River narrow, they form a 90 m plunge that ends in a series of swirling rock pools below. The area surrounding the waterfall is a national park where visitors can find an interesting selection of mammals, birds and plants, many of which are adapted to the harsh semi-arid climate.

THE ORANGE RIVER

This large river offers holiday-makers a range of exciting activities. Here are some options.

Between Onseepkans and Noordoewer

On the stretch of the Orange between Onseepkans and Noordoewer, canoe and rafting trips are an extremely

popular activity. Highlights include passing through most spectacular rocky, mountainous landscapes and nights sleeping out under the stars (www.felixunite.com).

Between Kakamas and Upington

The area around the section of road that tracks the river between Kakamas and Upington is fast becoming an important wine-producing region. While the area is not quite up there with the Cape wine routes, this region still offers something that wine fundis can get excited over. The Ebenaeser Guest House (www.augrabies-falls.com), a delightful country home set among vineyards on the outskirts of Kakamas, is the place to base yourself.

Riemvasmaak

Further along the Orange River lies the community-owned and -run concession of Riemvasmaak (www.greenkalahari. co.za; www.northerncape.org.za/riemvasmaak), which was one of the first land restitution projects undertaken by the new government after 1994. Having been forcibly removed in the early 1970s, hundreds of Nama, Xhosa and Damara families were allowed back to claim their heritage. The communities have since opened a section of the land to ecotourism, and they run a fantastic campsite with numerous self-catering chalets set amidst the rugged mountains. It is an incredible value-for-money getaway, and mountain bikers and hikers will find it particularly worthwhile.

Zulu dancers from a nearby village perform at Isibindi Zulu Lodge in the KwaZulu-Natal Midlands.

KwaZulu-Natal Midlands

The Midlands encompass the interior regions of KwaZulu-Natal, with specific emphasis on the towns that comprise the Battlefields Route and those strung out along the R103, the alternative route to the main N3 toll road.

THE BATTLEFIELDS

Prior to the apartheid era, the defining period in South Africa's history was the 70-year period during the 1800s when various wars and conflicts took place across the country. They were fierce and brutal battles that ended up shaping the destiny of the region, the country and the groups involved (www.anglozuluwar.com; www.battlefields.kzn.org.za; www.amajubaexperience.co.za).

Of the major battles, the first, the Battle of Blood River, took place in 1838 when the Boer leader Andries Pretorius led a commando against the Zulus in revenge for the massacre of Piet Retief. In the ensuing battle on the banks of the Mulaudzi River, fewer than 500 Boers held off repeated attacks by more than 10 000 Zulu warriors. On the morning of 16 December, after failing to penetrate the Boer laager and taking heavy casualties in the process, the Zulus retreated. History records that more than 3 000 Zulus were killed, while only three Boers were wounded.

The second major conflict took place in January 1879, when the Battle of Isandlwana and the Battle of Rorke's Drift were fought between the British and the Zulus. At Isandlwana, more than 1 300 British soldiers were killed after being ambushed by the Zulus. At Rorke's Drift, some of the survivors and a contingent of 139 men held off a 4 000-strong Zulu onslaught. Fighting went on through the night; only 17 British soldiers died. Eleven Victoria Crosses, Britain's highest military award, were subsequently handed out – the most ever for a battle in British history.

The last major wars of the 1800s were the two wars fought between the British and the Boers. The first Anglo-Boer War took place in 1880–81 when the Boers rose up against British rule and defeated them after a resounding victory in

ABOVE *Cleopatra Mountain Farmhouse is situated between the KwaZulu-Natal Midlands and the central regions of the uKhahlamba/Drakensberg mountains.*

the Battle of Majuba (www.amajubaexperience.co.za). The second war began in 1899 and ended with a British victory in 1902. Although both wars took place across South Africa, numerous defining events – the Siege of Ladysmith, for example – took place in the Midlands.

Battlefield routes

The various battlefield routes cover numerous historical towns – Newcastle, Dundee, Ladysmith and Vryheid being the main ones – and these are best explored by taking a self-drive trip, spending time in each town.

Another option would be to head for Isibindi Zulu Lodge (www.isibindiafrica.co.za), situated in Fugitive's Drift, a short drive from the two most famous battle sites, Isandlwana and Rorke's Drift. The lodge offers an extremely convenient and comfortable base from which to explore the surrounding historical sites, and can provide highly informative Zulu guides to accompany guests.

MIDLANDS MEANDER

The many country towns and farm villages found on the stretch of the R103 that winds its way between Pietermaritzburg and Estcourt together make up the region that is marketed as the Midlands Meander (www.kzn.org.za). Set amidst rolling hills and neatly worked farm fields, the appeal here is all about country living. Visitors to places like Mooi River, Nottingham Road, Balgowan, Dargle, Howick, Hilton and Hidcote will find much in the way of local arts and crafts, antique outlets, restaurants, home-made food products and outdoor activities to keep them occupied (www.meander-activities.com).

The uKhahlamba/ Drakensberg range

Stretching almost the entire length of southern Africa, the Great Escarpment covers almost 5 000 km from eastern Zimbabwe to the southern regions of the Eastern Cape, including the Maloti mountains of Lesotho. The escarpment's most celebrated section is the uKhahlamba/Drakensberg range, the stretch that dominates the entire western boundary of KwaZulu-Natal along the border with Lesotho. The mountains are not to be confused with the uKhahlamba-Drakensberg Park, a World Heritage Site that contains the mountains as well as all the reserves and wilderness areas associated with the mountains. The park was declared a heritage site in 2000 in recognition of its outstanding natural beauty and immense collection of rock art paintings.

With numerous peaks and buttresses reaching above 3 000 m and long stretches of granite walls with towering cliffs, sharp cutbacks and grassy spurs, the mountains are a true highland wonderland for outdoor enthusiasts, particularly hikers and climbers. Almost every lodge, hotel and campsite in the greater region caters for these activities and can give visitors updated information on the weather, preferable routes and specific precautions. Note, nevertheless, that the mountains can be dangerous, with extreme weather conditions not uncommon. High levels of rainfall, snowfalls and freezing temperatures are recorded throughout the year.

For ease of planning, the uKhahlamba/Drakensberg can be broken into four sectors.

NORTHERN SECTOR

This sector (www.cdic.co.za) includes the Royal Natal National Park, Thukela Falls and Cathedral Peak. This region

has arguably the most impressive scenery and some of the best hiking and climbing trails. For accommodation, visitors can choose between either lodge and self-catering options inside the park (www.kznwildlife.com) or the very comfortable Berg House and Cottages (www.wheretostay.co.za/theberghouse), situated between Bergville and the park gate. The property offers a variety of options and has the most glorious views looking onto the mountains.

CENTRAL SECTOR

This sector (www.cdic.co.za) includes Giant's Castle, Champagne Castle, Cathkin Peak and Monk's Cowl. Easier access and a greater variety of options make this section the most popular amongst hikers and outdoor enthusiasts. The outstanding lodge here is Cleopatra Mountain Farmhouse (www.cleomountain.com) situated a short distance from Giant's Castle. It's a large property with a wonderfully restored farmhouse encircled by 11 superb bedrooms, all with pleasant views of the surrounding mountains. The lodge is best known for its exceptional cuisine and excellent wine cellar.

SOUTHERN SECTOR

This sector is centred on the small villages of Underberg and Himeville and the legendary Sani Pass (www.drakensberg.

org; www.majoradventures.com). Head for Himeville rather than Underberg, as it is smaller, with a more charming atmosphere, and base yourself at the Plum Tree Lodge (www.plumtreelodge.com). A trip up the pass is absolutely worthwhile, and don't forget your passport as the pass forms the border between South Africa and Lesotho.

NORTHERN EASTERN CAPE SECTOR

The northern Eastern Cape sector is dominated by the Witteberge range, which wraps around Lesotho's southern border with South Africa. The towns of Barkly East, Lady Grey and Rhodes are to be found in the foothills.

Tiffindell (www.tiffindell.co.za), South Africa's only ski resort, is on the south-facing slopes, about 22 km from Rhodes (www.rhodesvillage.co.za). Scenically, the region is the most impressive of all the uKhahlamba/Drakensberg options, and the air is crispest, the mountain views clearest and the local folk friendliest.

The Wartrail New England (www.wartrail.co.za) corner, lying right below the main massif, is one of South Africa's most picturesque regions. There are several wonderful cottages to rent, with Millard Mountain Lodge (www.millardlodge.co.za) being amongst the best of them. Winter is particularly appealing, but be warned, it can get extremely cold.

Eastern Cape coast

This section of South Africa's coastline comprises two distinct regions – the Sunshine Coast and the Wild Coast – with the latter being the prize destination.

THE SUNSHINE COAST

This region (www.sunshinecoast-marketing.co.za) incorporates approximately 350 km of coastline between the cities of Port Elizabeth (www.nmbt.co.za; www.bluewaterbay.co.za) in the west and East London (www.eastlondonsa.com) in the east.

Beaches and ocean

With wonderfully temperate climates, the coastal stretch of the R72 linking the two cities is all about great beaches and ocean sports. The pick of the spots are the Woody Cape Nature Reserve (www.ecparks.co.za), Kenton on Sea (www.kenton.co.za), Port Alfred (www.portalfred.co.za) and the tiny seaside towns of Kleinemonde, Hamburg and Mpekweni.

Private reserves

The region has numerous private reserves for wildlife, with the best being the Sibuya Game Reserve (www.sibuya.co.za). Situated on the Kariega estuary, upriver from Kenton on Sea, the privately owned reserve offers a choice of two rustic tented camps overlooking the river and plenty of great game-viewing, including sightings of white rhino. An upmarket option is the Oceana Beach and Wildlife Reserve (www.oceanareserve.com), just outside Port Alfred.

Grahamstown

Any trip to the Sunshine Coast during the last week of June and the first week of July should certainly include a detour to Grahamstown (www.grahamstown.co.za). Also known as the City of Saints – more than 40 churches and cathedrals are found here – the town has become known worldwide for the annual National Arts Festival (www.nafest.co.za). Showcasing the very best South African art, music and acting talents across all genres, the festival has become South Africa's arts-and-culture highlight.

THE WILD COAST

There is little to appreciate from the previous apartheid government, but one fortunate offshoot is the wonderful Wild Coast. Beginning just north of East London, it stretches all the way to Port Edward on the border of KwaZulu-Natal, and comprises a uniquely undeveloped section of rugged coastline. Previously demarcated as the so-called independent homeland of Transkei, this huge expanse of sea and sand remained rural and relatively culturally intact because it was out of bounds to the large chains of South African hotels. It is home to the Xhosa people, many of whom still live within the old tribal system. Although rapidly being replaced by rectangular buildings, traditional round Xhosa huts can still be seen dotted across the rolling hills. Sadly, the young adults tend to migrate to the cities for work and many of the communities are obviously comprised of babies, children and the

elderly. For visitors to this coast, interaction with the local people truly adds to their experience.

It is inadvisable to travel the Wild Coast without a hardy vehicle or a 4x4. There are a few badly maintained – though tarred – roads, but mostly roads are rough dirt access routes that wind down to the sea from the main N2.

Beach hotels

A distinctive feature of the Wild Coast is the old, rambling hotels that dominate the best beach spots along the coast. Many of these were built in the 1960s and 1970s. They were often not sufficiently maintained during the homeland days but have recently been restored to provide comfortable old-style holidays for families, where parents don't have to give meals a thought.

BELOW *Rhinos seen up close at private Sibuya Game Reserve in the Eastern Cape.*
OPPOSITE *Hole-in-the-Wall outside Coffee Bay is the most well-known landmark along the Wild Coast.*

Washing day outside Coffee Bay on the Wild Coast in the Eastern Cape.

Hikes

Many of the beach hotels in the south have been given a new lease on life since being incorporated as overnight stops into the two very popular Wild Coast hikes: The Wild Coast Amble and the Wild Coast Meander (www.wildcoastholidays.co.za). Tackling one of these immensely enjoyable hikes for a few days is a great way to experience the Wild Coast.

Nature reserves

There are three stunning nature reserves on the Wild Coast managed by Eastern Cape Nature. All have rustic cabins and camping options.

Dwesa/Cwebe Nature Reserve – One of the most beautiful sections of the whole coastline, accessed by the tarred Willowvale Road, this reserve begins just a half-hour walk along the beach from the mouth of the Nqabarha River (www.ecparks.co.za). It stretches north to the Mbhashe River, which is overlooked by the rolling lawns of the old but characterful Haven Hotel (www.havenhotel.co.za).

Hluleka Nature Reserve – This reserve is accessed via the old Transkei's capital city, Mthatha.

ABOVE *Xhosa women head home after a day shopping at Hole-in-the-Wall on the Wild Coast.*

Mkambati Nature Reserve – Even further north is this stunning reserve, home to one of the world's only freshwater waterfalls that pour out into the ocean.

Bulungula Lodge

Perched on the headland between river mouth and sea, this innovative lodge and backpacker stop is a superb example of a community-owned project. A very worthwhile destination, the lodge is based on the design of the round Xhosa hut, but with added flair and fun. The project's originator has involved and consulted the local people, given them ownership, and facilitates the development of their local businesses without enriching himself in any way. This is a truly authentic and unique success story (www.bulungula.com).

Coffee Bay and Port St Johns

The only two small communities on the coastline, Coffee Bay and Port St Johns, provide great holiday destinations.

The Hole-in-the-Wall, just south of Coffee Bay, is a spectacular rock formation weathered by sea and sand. Don't miss this sight. The surrounding swimming, snorkelling and hiking are fantastic.

The holiday hub of Coffee Bay is fun and has a range of accommodation options, ranging from the Ocean View Hotel (www.oceanview.co.za) to a number of backpackers' establishments (www.coffeeshack.co.za). High up in the hills, with spectacular 180-degree views across the rolling landscape and down to the sea, is Raptor's View. This rambling and rustic little lodge has been lovingly handcrafted with recycled materials, and offers the best meals between Coffee Bay and Hole-in-the-Wall (Tel: +27 47 575-0308).

Port St Johns has the greatest variety of accommodation and activities along this coast. Noteworthy options include the Cremorne Estate, offering cabins and camping on the banks of the unspoilt Mzimvubu River (www.cremorne.co.za); the funky Jungle Monkey, which has spectacular views of mountain and sea (www.junglemonkey.co.za); and, just outside Port St Johns, the award-winning Umngazi River Bungalows and Spa (www.umngazi.co.za) – the Wild Coast's most sophisticated resort.

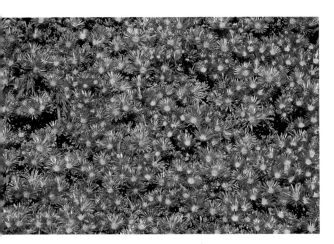

ABOVE *One of South Africa's wonders is the spring floral display of the West Coast and Namaqualand.*
OPPOSITE *The beaches of the West Coast are lapped by the Benguela Current's icy waters, which sweep northwards from the Southern Ocean.*

West Coast and Namaqualand

From on top of Table Mountain one can so easily see the extraordinary contrast between Cape Town, its immediate surrounding areas and the West Coast. While all else is green and mountainous, the West Coast is comparatively flat and dry. Some may find this coastline too bleak and desolate, but many are drawn by its relatively undeveloped state and its spaciousness. The cold Atlantic Ocean brings in thick ocean fog that may add to an eerie atmosphere, but it also carries much-needed moisture, which supports an amazing floral and faunal wonderland.

The Afrikaans folk who have inhabited the farms along this coastal area have, over the generations, developed a unique culture, accent and way of life. Although the area was traditionally a conservative and right-wing stronghold, the people are known for their warm hospitality and evenings of *braaivleis* (barbeques), beer and great storytelling.

The little fishing communities that have sprung up along the coast have served as recreational spots for these local farmers. The architecture is often rather haphazard and focuses more on function than form! Nevertheless, the sand is wondrously white, the sea is blue and the sky is endlessly clear.

A number of the best destinations along the West Coast are within an easy drive of Cape Town.

LANGEBAAN LAGOON AND SURROUNDS

The Langebaan lagoon, a haven for wind- and water-sport lovers (see the Travel South Africa chapter), is a favourite West Coast destination.

West Coast National Park

The West Coast National Park surrounds the Langebaan lagoon, which ensures that it will remain protected and pristine (www.sanparks.org).

Churchhaven

On a warm, cloudless day, this quaint village on the ocean side of the lagoon is quite paradisiacal.

PATERNOSTER

Further north, on a point, Paternoster is undoubtedly the West Coast's prettiest village. Traditionally a little fishing community, this collection of whitewashed cottages set against a dazzling blue sea, with colourful fishing boats lined up along the coves, makes for a picture-perfect sight (www. tourismcapewestcoast.co.za). Unfortunately, more recently developers and estate agents have discovered the town and a contemporary element has crept in.

LAMBERT'S BAY

This town is home to one of the world's largest Cape Gannet colonies. Bird Island Nature Reserve, linked to Lambert's Bay by the harbour wall, is managed by CapeNature, in collaboration with the local people, as a sustainable community

ABOVE *Recreational fishing is a favourite pastime in South Africa. This couple are out trying their luck on the Berg River in Velddrif.*

development project (www.capenature.org.za). The reserve provides protection to thousands of seabirds, not only the gannets, but also penguins and cormorants. These are best viewed from the rock hide, which allows the visitor an eye-to-eye encounter with these teeming colonies.

SPRING FLOWERS

One of South Africa's wonders is the spring floral display of the West Coast and Namaqualand. Towards the end of the winter, between August and October, the entire coastline and much of the West Coast's interior are transformed into spectacular carpets of wild blooms.

Inland and coastal flowers vary significantly. The coastal strip offers Strandveld shrublands and daisies. On the clay soils of the Swartland, the Renosterveld shrubland dominates. The mountainous region of the Cederberg has a typical mix of fynbos, with proteas, ericas and restios.

In years when the winter rainfalls are particularly good, the splendour of the floral colours is beyond anything a visitor could ever have imagined. For updates on the flower season see: www.tourismcapetown.co.za; www.northerncape.org.za

THE CEDERBERG

Inland of the coast, between Citrusdal and Clanwilliam, stretches a rugged and remote mountain range known as the Cederberg (www.capenature.org.za).

Hiking and rock climbing

These peaks and rocky outcrops entice rock climbers and hikers from all over the globe. The unusual geological formations make for some spectacular photography. Hikers and climbers can stay in the cabins or at the campsite at Algeria.

Remote hamlets

There are some lonely and tricky 4x4 routes through these mountains, accessing remote little hamlets and old mission

stations, where isolated families have lived for generations. Among these, Wuppertal, Rietpoort and Goedverwacht are worth a visit.

Plants, animals and rock art

Bushman's Kloof Wilderness Reserve and Retreat (www.bushmanskloof.co.za) is a five-star sanctuary, boasting a malaria-free wilderness experience, including fascinating indigenous flora, animal sightings and trips to see some of the 130 San rock art sites in the reserve.

ABOVE *The Cederberg range is one of a number of ranges that make up the Cape Fold mountains in the Western and Eastern Cape provinces.*
LEFT *A colony of gannets at Lambert's Bay on the West Coast.*

on SAFARI

While South Africa cannot boast extensive tracts of open or semipristine wilderness such as those that occur in other African countries, including Botswana, Zambia, Zimbabwe and Tanzania, it does have the most organised and efficient safari industry on the continent. A well-developed transport and tourism infrastructure links 21 national parks, a host of marine reserves and provincial game reserves and some of the most acclaimed private destinations on the African continent. Because of the climate mix and the variety of habitats, South Africa also has a remarkably high level of biodiversity that covers all classes of plants and animals.

Safari options

To get the very best out of a safari experience, visitors should approach their planning with more imagination than simply following the clichéd marketing spin that focuses on the Big Five: lion, leopard, rhino, elephant and buffalo. South Africa has so much more to offer. If it's a truly remote wildlife experience with a degree of privacy that you are after, your best options are the extreme north of the Kruger National Park; parts of the Kgalagadi Transfrontier Park; various walking trails in national parks, reserves and private concessions; and some of the private reserves.

The options and experiences that are available can be classified into the three broad categories.

GOVERNMENT-MANAGED NATIONAL PARKS

The national parks offer a variety of accommodation options from campsites to self-catering bungalows and, in a few cases, upmarket private lodgings managed by private companies which hold leases over given areas. South African National Parks (SANParks) is the official authority tasked with managing these national parks.

The larger parks usually have public restaurants and some form of shopping and fuel facility. Bookings — except for the private lodges and camps — are made through a central reservations system or at the gates. It is advisable to make bookings for the larger parks through the reservations system prior to travel. The government-run camps and lodges are often large and can be extremely busy during holiday periods, including school holidays.

PROVINCIAL PARKS AND RESERVES

Each of the nine provinces has a number of game reserves and nature reserves that are managed by the various provincial governments. These parks and reserves offer a variety of accommodation options from campsites to large hotels and lodges. Some of the larger reserves have restaurants, shops and fuel facilities. Bookings are made through a central reservations system run by the respective provinical governments. Some of the hotels and lodges can be extremely busy during holiday periods.

The most important provincial agencies are:
Ezemvelo KwaZulu-Natal Wildlife — www.kznwildlife.com
CapeNature — www.capenature.org.za
Mpumalanga Parks Board — www.mpumalangaparksboard. com
Limpopo Tourism & Parks — www.golimpopo.com
Eastern Cape Parks Board — www.ecparks.co.za
North West Parks — www.tourismnorthwest.co.za

PRIVATE GAME RESERVES AND CONCESSIONS

These often adjoin well-known national parks and reserves, and generally offer a more private and exclusive safari option that comes at a higher price. Some are international award-winning establishments that cater for the super-luxury end of the market. Reservations are made through each individual operator or lodge, although in some instances reservations can be made upon arrival.

PREVIOUS PAGES *Elephants are the feature attraction of the Addo Elephant National Park.*

OPPOSITE *Lions are still found in almost all parks and reserves in South Africa.*

Wildlife highlights

- South Africa is regarded as having the third highest — after Brazil and Indonesia — level of species diversity on the planet, and is one of only 17 countries ranked as being 'megadiverse'. The richly diverse Cape Floral Kingdom is a significant contributor to this status.
- While covering less than 1 per cent of the earth's surface, South Africa has more than 22 000 plant species — this represents 10 per cent of the world's total. There are 227 species of mammal, 851 of bird, 286 of amphibian, 77 500 of invertebrate, 112 of freshwater fish and 2 150 of marine fish described.

ABOVE *Adult elephants eat, on average, more than 150 kg of food in a 24-hour cycle.*

- For botanists and flower lovers, visiting the Cape Floral Kingdom, or fynbos biome, in the Western Cape, is a must. Covering a mere 0.04 per cent of the earth's surface, it is the smallest of the six recognised kingdoms of plants. But it is also the most diverse, with 8 700 species, of which more than 65 per cent are endemic.
- For sightings of the large cats, visiting particular spots can be fruitful. The Kruger National Park, Kgalagadi Transfrontier

Park and various private reserves – such as Sabi Sand, Timbavati, Madikwe, Phinda and Tswalu – are best for lion. While they occur in many of the national parks, leopard sightings in the Sabi Sand and Timbavati have become legendary. Cheetah are not commonly seen anywhere in South Africa, but the best chances are in the Kruger National Park, Kgalagadi Transfrontier Park, Phinda and the private reserves of Mpumulanga.

- Because South Africa has been at the forefront of rhinoceros conservation over the last three decades, it is the best place to see these animals. Sightings of both black rhino and white rhino are common in selected parks and reserves. Kruger National Park, Hluhluwe-Imfolozi Game Reserve, Pilanesberg Game Reserve, Sabi Sand and Timbavati offer the best options.
- Elephant are commonly seen in most of the larger national parks and private reserves, with Kruger National Park, Addo Elephant National Park, Pilanesberg Game Reserve, Sabi Sand and Timbavati being the best locations.
- The rare and endangered wild dog can be seen in the Kruger National Park, Hluhluwe-Imfolozi Game Reserve and various private reserves such as Sabi Sand, Timbavati and Madikwe.
- Spotted hyena are likely to be encountered in all the larger parks and reserves, while the more elusive brown hyena can be seen in the Kgalagadi Transfrontier Park and Tswalu Kalahari Reserve.
- A rich diversity of species of plains game can be seen in almost every national park and reserve. The endangered Cape mountain zebra is best viewed in the Mountain Zebra National Park. The rare roan and sable antelope can be seen in the Kruger National Park and oryx in the Kgalagadi Transfrontier Park and Tswalu.
- The largest population of buffalo is to be found in the Kruger National Park and the adjoining private reserves. Buffalo also occur in many of the other parks and reserves, but in far lower numbers.
- During August to late November, the southern Cape coast offers superb whalw-watching, particularly for southern right and humpback whales. Hermanus, Gansbaai and Plettenberg Bay are the most popular viewing locations, while the Whale Trail through the De Hoop Nature Reserve

offers a spectacular three-day option. These areas and the KwaZulu-Natal coast also have healthy populations of various dolphin species that are commonly seen from the shoreline.
- South Africa has an immensely rich avifauna, with a species list of 851 different birds, which include 58 endemics. While every wilderness area in the region offers a great birding experience, the provinces of KwaZulu-Natal, Mpumalanga and Limpopo carry the highest densities and species counts.
- South Africa's waters offer fantastic pelagic birding. Because the cold but nutrient-rich waters of the Benguela Current pass the southern tip of the African continent, the Cape coast has the greatest abundance and diversity of seabirds. More than 30 species have been recorded.
- The annual spring flower bloom that occurs in greater Namaqualand and parts of the Karoo is a spectacular sight. Depending on the rainfall patterns, the prime bloom period usually begins some time from mid-August and may last into late September.

A WORD OF CAUTION

Notwithstanding South Africa's notable conservation and wildlife-management achievements, there is also an unsavoury component that involves the captive breeding of large predators and various species of plains game, and the practice of canned hunting.

Carried out mostly on private farms and reserves, these practices are aimed at satisfying the international trophy-hunting industry. Certain species are bred for selected characteristics, and they are shot in cages or confined areas. The majority of these farms are to be found in the provinces of Free State, Limpopo, North West, Gauteng and Eastern Cape. Because there is a host of illegal and unethical practices associated with canned hunting and captive breed-ing, government and various private sector organisations are involved in an initiative to have these industries closed down. It is important to be aware that most of these operators attempt to mask their practices by conveying some form of a conservation or scientific message to unsuspecting visitors. If you become aware of these practices, report your experience to any recognised conservation agency.

FACT FILE))

South African National Parks

The core focus of South African National Parks (SANParks), in managing the country's 21 national parks, is on biodiversity conservation, building relationships with and uplifting communities surrounding the parks, and sustainable tourism. The conservation component is run by the Conservation Services Department: various units deal with scientific issues, transfrontier conservation, veterinary services, and it has many smaller research units and centres.

In total, the parks cover approximately four million ha of arid, coastal, mountain and bushveld habitats. Fifteen of them offer accommodation options within the gates, while the rest have private facilities on their outskirts. SANParks continues to purchase land surrounding existing parks with the aim of increasing terrestrial protected areas to 8 per cent and marine protected areas to 20 per cent of South Africa by 2010.

SANParks manages the following 21 national parks and marine reserves:

	Park size (ha)	First proclaimed
Addo Elephant National Park	163 970	1931
Agulhas National Park	5 690	1999
Augrabies Falls National Park	41 676	1966
Bontebok National Park	2 786	1931
Camdeboo National Park	14 500	2005
Golden Gate Highlands National Park	11 633	1963
Karoo National Park	77 094	1979
Kgalagadi Transfrontier Park	959 103	1931
Knysna National Lake Area	15 000	1985
Kruger National Park	1 962 362	1898
Mapungubwe National Park	5 356	1989
Marakele National Park	50 726	1993
Mokala National Park	19 611	2007
Mountain Zebra National Park	24 663	1937
Namaqua National Park	103 000	1999
IAi-IAis/Richtersveld Transfrontier Park	162 445	1991
Table Mountain National Park	24 310	1998
Tankwa Karoo National Park	43 899	1986
Tsitsikamma National Park	63 942	1964
West Coast National Park	36 273	1985
Wilderness National Park	10 600	1985

CONTACT DETAILS FOR SANPARKS

Central Reservations – P.O. Box 787, Pretoria, South Africa 0001; Tel: +27 12 428-9111; e-mail: reservations@sanparks.org

Satellite Reservation Offices – Johannesburg Tel: +27 11 678-8870; Cape Town Tel: +27 21 487-6800; Durban Tel: +27 31 304-4934; Bloemfontein Tel: +27 51 430-6781; Nelspruit Tel: +27 13 755-1988

Administration – Tel: +27 12 426-5000

Travel Trade – Tel: +27 12 426-5025; e-mail: traveltrade@sanparks.org

Websites – www.sanparks.org; www.parks-sa.co.za

GO WILD

The Wild Card is a smart-card loyalty programme recently introduced to benefit regular visitors to the listed national parks and various provincially managed game reserves and nature reserves. The system is linked to more than 2 000 retail and service provider partners, which contribute to the reward scheme through discounts and cashback rewards.

Usage of the Wild Card helps SANParks by subsidising conservation initiatives.

Contacts for Wild Card enquiries and benefits —
Tel: +27 12 428-9111 or +27 86 123-4002;
e-mail: wild@infinityrewards.co.za; www.sanparks.org or www.wildinafrica.com

Parks and reserves

KRUGER NATIONAL PARK

The Kruger National Park (KNP) is South Africa's flagship wilderness area and has, over the last century, been one of Africa's most well-known reserves for wildlife. Although Paul Kruger proclaimed the zone between the Sabie and Crocodile rivers as a protected sanctuary in 1898, it became formally

ABOVE *Visitors take a guided walk through the fever tree forests in the Pafuri region of the Kruger National Park.*

known as the KNP only in 1926, with the amalgamation of various smaller reserves. Its size has increased substantially since then and, at 19 633 sq km (1.96 million ha), it is South Africa's largest park and one of the largest on the African continent. It is also the busiest, with almost 1.3 million visitors passing through its gates annually. This represents approximately 60 per cent of the total number of visitors to South Africa's 21 national parks and between 75 per cent and 80 per cent of SANParks's annual income.

To many South Africans, the KNP has become something of an institution and it is viewed as South Africa's most treasured natural asset. The annual camping holiday, or one-week stay in a self-catering bungalow, are still rituals enjoyed by very many families. A plus is that it's affordable and convenient, and the game- and bird- viewing are usually immensely rewarding. The park's biodiversity includes 147 mammal species, 507 species of bird, 114 species of reptile and 336 species of tree. Six river systems feed into 16 distinct ecozones. The park carries South Africa's largest populations of elephant, white rhinoceros, buffalo, giraffe and, amongst the predators, lion, leopard and wild dog. Although rare species such as roan and sable antelope, tsessebe and Lichtenstein's hartebeest occur, they are seldom seen.

The park is renowned as a world leader in environmental practices and conservation initiatives, with many of the country's best biological scientists having spent time at Skukuza, the park's headquarters. The most recent initiative has been the establishment of the Great Limpopo Transfrontier Park, which incorporates conservation areas of Zimbabwe and Mozambique adjoining the KNP. The concept is based on the idea of creating expanded conservation areas and introducing new tourism infrastructure in a manner beneficial to both the wildlife and neighbouring traditional communities.

Despite these successes, park management has also drawn its fair share of criticism over the years. The past and proposed elephant-culling programmes have as many detractors as they do proponents, and the annual wildlife sales – which see rhino and elephant sold to the canned-hunting industry – are regarded as irresponsible. The park's fencing, fire and water-hole policies are always under close scrutiny, as is management's more recent attitude to awarding private concessions within a national park.

Going forward, a major challenge will be settling the various outstanding land claims the park faces. Almost 50 per cent of the park is under some form of claim, with the largest ones being near Punda Maria and Phalaborwa in the north, and a number of smaller claims being on land at Skukuza and various other camps.

Where to stay

Part of the KNP's appeal is its successful year-round game-viewing. Because of accessibility, the diversity of habitats and the best sightings of rhino, the southern camps – such as Skukuza, Pretoriuskop, Lower Sabie and Crocodile Bridge – are the most popular.

Those seeking a little less bustle head north, as the closer one gets to the Limpopo River, the less congestion one experiences. In the central regions, Satara offers great all-round game-viewing and Olifants is a fantastic stop as it has the most scenic setting of all the camps. In the north, Punda Maria offers a smaller and more remote setting.

Various private concessions are spread throughout the park, all offering a greater degree of privacy and luxury. Of these, the two lodges in the Tinga Private Game Lodge (www.tinga.co.za), Legends Lodge and Narina Lodge, are great options in the southwestern region. Both overlook the Sabie River, with Legends having a more colonial feel and Narina being distinctly more African in its design. At the very top end of the luxurious options in the KNP are the Singita lodges (www.singita.com), Lebombo and Sweni. Both are situated in a private concession in the southeast, bordering Mozambique. Lebombo has won a number of international design awards with its cutting-edge contemporary style, while Sweni has a more traditional safari feel.

Arguably, the ultimate KNP experience, though, is the private wilderness area of Pafuri (www.wilderness-safaris. com) in the far north. Recently awarded to the Makuleke people in a successful land claim, it lies between the Luvuvhu and Limpopo rivers and with its unique fever tree forests, it has the most stunning scenery found anywhere in the park. Wilderness Safaris has become the community's chosen partner for ecotourism and, from Pafuri Camp, which overlooks the river, this company runs a range of activities that include walking and birding.

An alternative activity for the more adventurous involves joining one of the extremely popular Wilderness Trails. Usually run over four days, the trails are based in a number of different private areas, with walkers returning to their small rustic camps each night.

HLUHLUWE-IMFOLOZI GAME RESERVE

This game reserve is generally regarded as KwaZulu-Natal's premier wilderness destination. First proclaimed back in 1895, it is one of the oldest protected areas in Africa. Prior to being accorded this formal status, the region enjoyed a more traditional form of protection, as it was the exclusive hunting preserve of the Zulu kings.

ABOVE *An early morning game drive in the Hluhluwe-Imfolozi Game Reserve is a must for visitors.*

Today, the reserve covers 96 000 ha and includes a wide variety of habitats that are home to 80 species of mammal, including the densest concentration of black rhino per square kilometre in the world, and more than 300 bird species. It is also world renowned for its successful rhino conservation initiatives, first launched in the 1950s as 'Operation Rhino'. Imfolozi will forever be known as the place that saved the white rhino from extinction, as this reserve was established primarily as a sanctuary for this once-threatened species.

Where to stay

While there are various lodge and camp options run by the wildlife authorities, Hilltop Camp in Hluhluwe and Mpila Camp in Imfolozi are the prime choices (www.kznwildlife.com). The most magical way to experience this park is on foot with the Wilderness Leadership School (see page 142).

ISIMANGALISO WETLAND PARK

Formerly known as the Greater St Lucia Wetland Park, iSimangaliso Wetland Park is situated on the northeastern coastal plains of KwaZulu-Natal, stretching from the Mozambique border in the north to the town of Maphelana in the south. Covering 3 280 sq km, this wetland and dune complex was declared South Africa's first natural World Heritage Site in 1999. Lying a mere 275 km north of Durban, the park is also the most popular wilderness destination in KwaZulu-Natal.

The region is divided into three sections: Kosi Bay, Lake Sibaya and Sodwana Bay in the north; Lake St Lucia, Cape Vidal and Mkhuze in the central region; and Mission Rocks and the St Lucia Estuary in the south. The alternating rise and fall in sea levels over time has resulted in the distinct

The Wilderness Leadership School

To date, more than 50 000 people have walked a trail with the Wilderness Leadership School (WLS), and the vast majority of them express similar sentiments: they highlight the inspirational aspects of the school's minimum-impact walking and camping trails, and the sense of spiritual renewal and reflection that comes from days immersed in the trail. Within Africa, few organisations truly espouse and practise better than the school does the principles of simplicity and natural spirituality in the wilderness.

The WLS was founded in 1957 by the world-renowned conservationist and naturalist Dr Ian Player and his close friend Magqubu Ntombela. They established the nonprofit educational trust with the idea of introducing people from all walks of life to the wonders of the natural world. For them, and all the great guides that have worked at the WLS over the decades, their mission has been to 'bring about a realisation of the interdependence of all things, especially between the human and the nonhuman elements of the earth'. The trails also provide the opportunity for participants to 'deepen their understanding of their spiritual being, their relationship to other humans and their place within the Earth's greater community of life'.

Trails are run over a number of days in the southern regions of Hluhluwe-Imfolozi Game Reserve. Guests carry their own packs and food for the trail. In today's safari world, where fanfare and glitz have become the features of marketing the industry, the WLS approach is a most refreshing reminder of what the essence of wilderness is actually about. To book a trail through the WLS, go to www.wildernesstrails.org.za, or e-mail wilderness.trails@eastcoast.co.za

ABOVE *The most magical way to experience the Hluhluwe-Imfolozi Game Reserve in KwaZulu-Natal is on foot with the Wilderness Leadership School.*

network of linked geographical features that include long, sandy beaches, coral reefs, swamp forests, estuaries, freshwater wetlands, grass plains and coastal dune forest and a shoreline that is now more than 150 m below its level of approximately 140 million years ago. The St Lucia estuary is the largest estuarine system in Africa and the coral reefs off Sodwana are the southernmost on the continent.

These habitats are home to more than 500 bird species and several mammal species, including rhino, buffalo, elephant and hippo. The coastal waters remain crucial breeding grounds for various whale and turtle species.

Where to stay

The greater region offers a myriad different accommodation options. The towns of Hluhluwe, St Lucia and Sodwana have a selection of B&Bs and hotels, while there are various lodge and campsite options along the coast and on the inland lakes. Activities include fishing, diving, walking, boating, kayaking and game- and bird-viewing.

If you enjoy horse riding, the most exciting of the activities is riding in the wilderness. Bhangazi Horse Safaris (www. horsesafari.co.za), operating out of St Lucia, offers privately guided riding safaris that includes beach and bush day-rides within the park, as well as multi-day camping safaris in the big game areas of the Eastern Shores and the Tewate Wilderness area. A six-night safari is highly recommended, although shorter options are available. All rides and safaris are led by experienced guides and back-up riders. Two styles of overnight safari are on offer, both in mobile tented camps that move to accommodate the game-viewing and the conditions. The 'Adventure Safaris' are basic but comfortable and allow for a genuine old-style African adventure. The more luxurious 'True Safari' is a fully catered, colonial-style affair. Traversing the wilderness and experiencing African wildlife on horseback has to be one of the highlights of a trip to South Africa.

Of the coastal destinations, the outstanding one is Rocktail Bay (www.wilderness-safaris.com). Situated in Maputaland along the far northern coastline between Sodwana Bay and Kosi Bay, Rocktail Bay offers the very best of everything. The diving in the Maputaland Marine Reserve is unparalleled in South Africa and the summertime turtle-breeding season is a particularly memorable feature of Rocktail Bay.

ABOVE *Bhangazi Horse Safaris conducts riding trails through various sectors of the iSimangaliso Wetland Park.*

ADDO ELEPHANT NATIONAL PARK

This is the leading national park in the Eastern Cape and it also happens to be one of the best family-orientated safari destinations in the country. Because of its proximity to Port Elizabeth and its malaria-free status, it is an obvious addition to the itinerary of people visiting the Garden Route. Its 164 000 ha cover five distinct biomes that include the Zuurberg mountains, the Sundays River and the marine section of Colchester and Woody Cape. Originally proclaimed in 1931 as a sanctuary for the last 11 elephant in the region, the park has since been expanded on a number of occasions and is now home to almost 500 elephant. The park also carries herds of buffalo and zebra as well as black rhino and numerous antelope species. The predators comprise modest populations of lion, leopard and hyena and a number of the smaller carnivore species. The most recent additions to the park have been the coastal sections and the offshore islands of St Croix and Bird Island, which means visitors can now add whales, dolphins and penguins to the list of attractions.

Where to stay

All accommodation options in Addo Elephant National Park are self-catering, and these range from camping and basic huts to luxury guesthouses (e-mail: addoenquiries@sanparks.org).

There are also a variety of private accommodation options, both inside the park and along its boundaries. Of these, Gorah Elephant Camp (www.hunterhotels.com), situated south of Addo Main Camp in a private concession, is the outstanding option. The Gorah farmhouse, which dates back to 1785, has been fabulously renovated by Hunter Hotels, retaining its original charm and providing a glorious retreat from which to enjoy the best of Addo Elephant National Park. The highlights of this venue must be relaxing on the wide verandah of the main house, enjoying the superb cuisine, and watching a herd of elephant or buffalo go about their business at the nearby water hole. Accommodation consists of 11 luxurious, *en suite* safari tents, each with a private deck looking onto the Gorah plains.

RIGHT *The water hole in front of Gorah Elephant Camp in the Addo Elephant National Park.*

ABOVE *The Cape mountain zebra is best seen by visiting the Mountain Zebra National Park in the Eastern Cape.*

MOUNTAIN ZEBRA NATIONAL PARK

First proclaimed in 1937 to save the Cape mountain zebra from extinction, this park has undergone numerous additions to its original size and now covers more than 24 000 ha of immensely scenic mountainous Karoo terrain. Although still listed as endangered, the Cape mountain zebra population of the park now stands at more than 300 animals.

The park is also well known for its population of black wildebeest, a species endemic to South Africa, and red hartebeest, blesbok, kudu, eland, buffalo and springbok are commonly seen.

Where to stay

Mountain Zebra National Park offers both camping and chalet options (e-mail: reservations@sanparks.org). The park is at its most impressive during the months of springtime, when the flowers are out. The park is situated in a malaria-free area.

Transfrontier Conservation Areas

For many in the world of conservation and wildlife management, the implementation of transfrontier conservation areas is the most promising solution to Africa's challenges of species and habitat conservation. Also known as 'corridor conservation' or mega-parks, the concept seeks to link national parks and wilderness areas that are found within close proximity of each other, regardless of international boundaries, into substantially larger cross-border areas.

Presently, 22 TFCAs have been identified, covering more than 475 000 sq km across 15 African countries. Two have already been formally designated and a further 10 are either in the discussion or implementation phase. The magnitude of the vision is underlined by the inclusion of 110 different national parks, game reserves and designated wildlife areas, representing 41 per cent of all formally protected regions within southern, eastern and central Africa.

The Peace Parks Foundation has become synonymous with the promotion and implementation of Transfrontier Conservation Areas (TFCAs) throughout Africa. Founded in 1997 in South Africa by the late Dr Anton Rupert of the Rembrandt Group, the foundation is now under the dedicated stewardship of Professor Willem van Riet and is based in Stellenbosch (www.peaceparks.org).

ABOVE *Oryx (gemsbok) grazing in the Kgalagadi Transfrontier Park, the subcontinent's first transfrontier park.*

KGALAGADI TRANSFRONTIER PARK

South Africa's first transfrontier park came about in 2000 when the Kalahari Gemsbok National Park (first proclaimed in 1931) and Botswana's Gemsbok National Park were combined to form a 3.7 million ha greater biome. Its vast size makes it the only park in South Africa that does not actively manage its wildlife populations. Lying centrally within the greater Kalahari region, the harsh semidesert terrain belies the extraordinary diversity of life that occurs within the park. The feature attractions are the largest concentration of cheetah in South Africa, healthy populations of lion and leopard, and the species – such as oryx, red hartebeest and springbok – typically found in these arid conditions.

Where to stay

The park has three main camps that offer a range of accommodation options, including large campsites, as well as fuel and shop facilities. Mata Mata is situated in the southwest corner along the Auob River, Nossob in the centre on the Nossob River, and Twee Rivieren, the main entrance and park headquarters, is located in the extreme south.

Over the last few years, the park has added various smaller, private accommodation options, and if the budgets allow, these are preferable to the main camps. Kielie Krankie in the dunes in the south of the park, Urikaruus along the Auob River and Grootkolk in the far north are good choices (e-mail: reservations@sanparks.org).

DR GUS MILLS »

Amongst the numerous world-renowned South African scientists and researchers working in the fields of conservation and biology, one of the most distinguished is Dr Gus Mills. Over the last 34 years he has contributed hugely to our knowledge and understanding of the region's carnivore populations, particularly the hyena species.

After completing a PhD in Wildlife Management, Gus spent 32 years working for SANParks, mainly in the Kgalagadi Transfrontier Park and the Kruger National Park, specialising in carnivore behavioural ecology and conservation. During this period, he was instrumental in establishing and running the Carnivore Conservation Group for the Endangered Wildlife Trust, and was Chairman of the IUCN Hyena Specialist Group and on the steering committees of the Canid Specialist Group and the Cat Specialist Group. He also authored two books on predators and one on the Kalahari, and was an editor of the *Complete Book of Mammals of South Africa*. His scientific work is supported by more than 100 papers published both locally and internationally, and he still acts as an Extraordinary Professor to the Mammal Research Institute of Pretoria University.

Presently, Gus is again based in the Kgalagadi, where he is the Research Fellow of The Tony and Lizette Lewis Foundation. With the financial support of the foundation, and in conjunction with SANParks, Gus and his wife Margie

are running the Kgalagadi Cheetah Project. This project is a five-year study that aims to identify the ecological role, behavioural adaptations, demographic parameters, and genetic and conservation status of this species. The cheetah is listed by the IUCN as vulnerable, and Gus believes the park's cheetah population is vital to the survival of the species in the greater region as it is one of South Africa's largest naturally functioning populations.

To donate funds to the Kgalagadi Cheetah Project or to find out more about its work, visit the project's website at www.tllf.org.za/cheetahs

DE HOOP NATURE RESERVE

The diversity of terrain covered by this 34 000 ha nature reserve is what makes De Hoop a particularly special destination. The reserve includes the Potberg mountains and some of the finest coastline that South Africa has to offer, from rocky shorelines, dramatic cliffs, blowholes, reefs and rock pools to endless, white, sandy beaches and rolling dunes.

The reserve conserves the largest tract of the Cape Floral Kingdom – the world's smallest and most threatened of the six plant kingdoms – and 86 species of mammal thrive in this landscape. Look out for the rare bontebok and Cape mountain zebra, as well as eland and grey rhebok. After dark you may even be rewarded with a rare sighting of caracal or leopard.

De Hoop is also well known for its variety of birds, both coastal and grassland, with more than 260 species recorded within the reserve. The De Hoop Vlei attracts large numbers of water birds and the last remaining breeding colony of rare Cape Vultures in the Western Cape is found in the Potberg. The reserve is also a good place to spot some of the regional endemic species with the Hottentot Buttonquail, Knysna Woodpecker, Agulhas Clapper Lark, Orange-breasted Sunbird, Cape Spurfowl, Cape Cormorant, Southern Tchagra and Cape Sugarbird being amongst the most sought after.

The Whale Trail, a five-day hike, is one of the country's pre-eminent hiking experiences. It is a superb hike, no matter what time of the year, but walking it during the winter whale-breeding season – when the chances of seeing southern right whales are great – may enhance your experience. Bookings for the winter months need to be made a year in advance (www.capenature.org.za).

Where to stay

There are a number of really fabulous self-catering accommodation options. Refer to the CapeNature website (www.capenature.org.za) for further information.

BAVIAANSKLOOF WILDERNESS AREA

The Baviaanskloof mega-reserve, until quite recently one of South Africa's best-kept wilderness secrets, lies hidden between the Kouga and Baviaanskloof mountain ranges.

It is a special place for many reasons, not least of which is that it forms an important part of a World Heritage Site, the

ABOVE *Chacma baboons are commonly seen in most national parks and reserves in South Africa.*

149

Cape Floral Kingdom. The reserve is not easily accessible as the road that runs the length of the Baviaanskloof valley is impossible to traverse by sedan vehicle. This road twists through spectacular mountain passes, red rock cliffs, narrow gorges and fertile valley floors.

An expanse of 189 000 ha of this impressive place currently falls within the Baviaanskloof Conservation Area, which is managed by the Eastern Cape Parks Board. This area is unspoiled, and its rugged terrain is home to a large variety of wildlife, including large herds of Cape buffalo, red hartebeest, kudu and Cape mountain zebra. Signs of leopard abound, although the cats themselves are rarely seen. The reserve's namesake, the baboon, is plentiful.

Where to stay

There are beautifully situated camping areas and some self-catering cottages within the reserve. For further information, go to www.ecparks.co.za. Some 4x4 trails off the main route take you up side gorges and over mountain peaks. To book one of these go to www.baviaans.co.za

A number of private landowners in the mega-reserve offer a variety of exciting accommodation options. The Sederkloof Lodge (www.sederkloof.co.za) is one such commendable place. This luxurious lodge offers fabulous meals and splendid comfort with breathtaking views of a remote side valley. For other private accommodation choices surf the Baviaans website given above or phone the Baviaans Tourism office (Tel: +27 44 923-1702 or +27 44 923-1921).

Best of the rest

Of the many other national and provincial parks and reserves, the ones listed below are certainly worth considering.

BONTEBOK NATIONAL PARK

With the Langeberg mountains as a backdrop and the Breede River forming the western boundary, this scenic park was proclaimed specifically to conserve the bontebok. Once numbering as few as 17 animals, they now number more than 3 000 and are no longer on the critically endangered list (www.sanparks.org).

ABOVE *One of many mountain streams that flow through the Baviaanskloof Wilderness Area.*
OPPOSITE *Because of commercial ostrich farming in South Africa, ornithologists now distinguish between wild populations and feral populations.*

TSITSIKAMMA NATIONAL PARK

This marine reserve forms part of the Garden Route and stretches along the Cape coast between Nature's Valley and Oyster Bay. The stunning beauty of this coastal region is best experienced by doing the Otter Trail, a five-day hike that meanders along the rugged shoreline and through the forests of Tsitsikamma (www.sanparks.org).

AUGRABIES FALLS NATIONAL PARK

The thundering 90-m-high Augrabies Falls on the Orange River is the main attraction here. The park covers 41 676 ha, and is situated on either side of the Orange River in the arid Northern Cape. The park carries small populations of springbok, oryx, klipspringer, black rhino and giraffe (www.sanparks.org).

MARAKELE NATIONAL PARK

Situated on the western edge of the Waterberg mountains, this park is a convenient and pleasing day or weekend option for those based in Gauteng. It offers a mix of great birding – its bird population includes one of the largest breeding colonies of Cape Vulture – and game-viewing. A variety of antelope species, elephant and rhino can also be seen (www.sanparks.org).

TANKWA KAROO NATIONAL PARK

This is one of the more recently proclaimed parks, which, being situated in the remote regions of the Karoo, offers a true desert escape for those in search of solitude. Dry and arid, this place is all about the rugged but striking Karoo landscapes and the smaller creatures that have adapted to the harsh conditions (www.sanparks.org).

TEMBE ELEPHANT GAME RESERVE

This small reserve, on the northern border between South Africa and Mozambique, offers great elephant viewing, and with a species list of almost 350, is a favourite with bird-watchers (www.kznwildlife.com).

PILANESBERG GAME RESERVE

This reserve is situated within an ancient volcanic complex that lies in the transition zone between the dry Kalahari and the Lowveld. The reserve is well stocked with a variety of

species of plains game as well as predators, and is within a few hours' drive of the major cities in Gauteng (www.pilanesberggamereserve.com).

The private reserves

In South Africa, the vast majority of land is owned by private companies and individuals on a freehold basis. South Africa's laws also allow for the private ownership of wildlife, which is bought and sold in most provinces, much like domestic livestock, on auctions and through private sales. The combination of these two factors has resulted in a dramatic growth of private game reserves over the last two decades.

SABI SAND PRIVATE GAME RESERVE AND TIMBAVATI PRIVATE NATURE RESERVE

These two private reserves are probably the most well-known tracts of private wilderness in the country, and their lodges and camps are regarded internationally as some of the finest in Africa.

Sabi Sand (http://sabi.krugerpark.co.za) was established in the 1950s when several private landowners decided to drop the fences of their respective properties to create a larger reserve. Timbavati (www.timbavati.com) was formed a decade or so later. Since those bold steps, the reserves have grown substantially. In 1993–94 the vision was completed when the main eastern boundary fence with the Kruger National Park (KNP) was dropped. This was done in the best interests of conservation and wildlife management. The private reserves have benefited from being part of a substantially greater wilderness area, and they are able to market themselves as part of the greater KNP.

Almost all the establishments within these reserves are aimed at the middle to luxury end of the market, and many people regard the safari experience offered here as being the very best South Africa has to offer. The wildlife, which includes almost every species on the regional mammal lists, is prolific and viewing game on drives tends to be effortless.

Where to stay

Sabi Sand Private Game Reserve – Mala Mala, Londolozi and Sabi Sabi – pioneers of extreme comfort, style, convenience and opulence in the bush – are the most established names in the Sabi Sand. They have more recently been joined by the likes of Singita, Lion Sands and Savanna, amongst others. **Timbavati Private Nature Reserve** – Ngala, Tanda Tula and Kings Camp are some of the best options.

PHINDA PRIVATE GAME RESERVE

The Phinda story tells of South Africa's most successful and celebrated conservation initiatives. Situated within the heart of the sand forest, wetland and savanna mosaic of Maputaland in KwaZulu-Natal, Phinda comprises 21 000 ha of rehabilitated farmland and surviving wilderness. It also lies within the iSimangaliso Wetland Park.

Of the many successful species reintroductions into Phinda, the most welcome have been those of the cheetah and white rhino. The reserve has also entered into numerous empowerment partnerships with surrounding communities. Recently, CC Africa, Phinda's managers, signed a ground-breaking agreement with local communities, settling a land claim on the reserve.

Besides the great game-viewing, Phinda is also a bird-watcher's paradise, particularly during the summer months. More than 400 species have been recorded, and the reserve offers great opportunities to spot specials such as the Pink-throated Twinspot, African Broadbill, Rudd's Apalis and Neergaard's Sunbird.

Where to stay

The reserve has six luxury lodges, most of which have won international recognition. They all offer sumptuous accommodation and cuisine. There is one smaller more rustic camp from which visitors can enjoy walking experiences (www.ccafrica.com).

MADIKWE GAME RESERVE

Madikwe Game Reserve lies in North West province along South Africa's border with Botswana. Developed in the early 1990s, this government initiative was created to relieve this economically depressed area. It is now a highly successful joint venture between the state, the private sector and the local communities.

This malaria-free destination is home to the big five and a vast selection of other wildlife. This is largely due to a world-renowned game-relocation project, which involved the successful introduction of more than 8 000 animals of 28 different species into the reserve.

Where to stay

The community-owned Buffalo Ridge Safari Lodge and Thakadu River Camp have inspiring stories of local community upliftment behind them. Both lodges are beautiful luxury camps built in great settings with décor that reflects the natural environment around them. They offer superb cuisine produced by chefs trained through an in-house programme developed for trainees from the local communities. To find out more about these lodges, contact the Madikwe Collection (Tel: +27 11 805-9995; www.madikwecollection.co.za).

For a fabulous safari with the family, Jaci's Safari Lodge and Jaci's Tree Lodge provide perfect venues. In close proximity to each other, these two lodges nestle comfortably amongst the trees of a riverine forest on the banks of the Marico River. The décor is colourful, clever and comfortable, making these lovingly handcrafted lodges stand out from the many others on offer in Madikwe (www.madikwe.com; e-mail: jaci@madikwe.com).

THE WATERBERG

This wilderness area, covering some 15 000 sq km in Limpopo province, incorporates a number of reserves, concessions and private farms and also a national park. It was aptly named the Waterberg by the early Voortrekkers due to the abundant supply of clear water delivered by springs and rivulets from the impressive mountain range. With its sheer rock faces and unusual sandstone and volcanic mix, the Waterberg plateau is the dominant feature of the landscape in the greater region. Its steep cliff faces are home to one of the few remaining breeding colonies of Cape Vultures.

ABOVE *Meal times on safari, especially in such stunning settings, are an integral part of the overall experience.*

The Waterberg is steeped in conservation history, with some of South Africa's most successful initiatives emerging from this area. These projects include the rehabilitation of old grazing lands back to wilderness, the development of species-protection programmes and the development of reserves and conservancies. In more recent times, the focus has been on removing old fences between reserves and farms in order to encourage the development of biodiversity.

One of the most awesome and powerful wildlife sightings to experience is a vicious confrontation between lions and hyenas. This one occurred in the Sabi Sand Private Game Reserve.

ABOVE *After a long and successful game drive, sundowner drinks are a welcome feature of safaris in the private game reserves.*

Where to stay

Lapalala Wilderness School and Reserve — This was founded in the early 1980s by well-known conservationists Clive Walker and Dale Parker (www.lapalala.com). Originally 19 different farms, the reserve was consolidated to form what is now a 36 000 ha tract of wilderness in various stages of rehabilitation. This provided the perfect site for breeding programmes for the endangered black rhino and roan antelope and the development of the famed wilderness school, where children come to learn about nature, the environment and their cultural heritage. Lapalala is now home to a large variety of wildlife, including both black and white rhino, buffalo, hippo, crocodile, leopard, baboon and a variety of antelope species. Lapalala also forms a significant part of the Waterberg Biosphere Reserve, proclaimed by UNESCO in 2001. There is an authenticity to Lapalala that is evident to its fortunate visitors. Guests are able to enjoy daily game drives and guided walks. Several accommodation options are available, with the more exclusive camps tucked away comfortably in the rugged landscape.

Marataba — At the other end of the Waterberg experience is Marataba, nestled on the edge of the Marakele National Park on the private Mara Concession. With its 15 exclusive air-conditioned tented suites, all with splendid views onto the Waterberg mountains, this lodge is the epitome of indulgent relaxation. As with all Hunter Hotels establishments, this is a lodge experience that will satisfy every safari fantasy (www.hunterhotels.com).

KWANDWE PRIVATE GAME RESERVE

Kwandwe, meaning 'place of the blue crane' in Xhosa, is a 22 000 ha malaria-free reserve that lies in the heart of the Eastern Cape and includes 30 km of the Great Fish River. Within a decade, what was formerly all farmland has been rehabilitated and transformed into one of South Africa's most successful conservation initiatives. Today, the reserve carries healthy populations of lion, cheetah, elephant, black rhino, white rhino, buffalo, and all the indigenous antelope species found in the region.

Where to stay

Catering to the luxury end of the market, the award-winning accommodation options include two traditional safari lodges and a restored historic farmhouse (www.ccafrica.com). All three are renowned for their excellent setting, fine cuisine stylish design and interiors.

Be guided

While selecting the best park or reserve and accommodation goes a long way to making for a memorable safari, the guide that you have with you will be the factor that ensures it can be a 'once in a lifetime' experience. Nearly all the well recognised private destinations have a number of trained guides – many of them with years of experience – that will accompany you. They are with you on activities and they sit with their guests at all meal times. The top establishments have strict criteria for training and testing their guides, and some of these guides have become recognised specialists in particular fields. This adds huge value to the overall learning experience while on safari. If you have friends who have travelled to the region, ask them, or get your agent to recommend a guide who will fit your particular interests and type of safari.

If you are booked into a government-run facility in the national parks, enquire about the services of private guides when booking or ask at the reception desk on arrival and they will be able to book a guide for you. The parks offer a range of guided activities which include game drives, bush walks and, in some cases, night drives.

If you wish for a strong educational and practical slant to your safari experience, then best you get hold of EcoTraining (www.ecotraining.co.za; Tel: +27 13 745-7777). Started in the early 1990s by two of South Africa's most experienced guides, the school is now the leading provider of nature-based training programmes and field-guide courses in southern Africa. Courses run from a few days to a full year, and cover a wide variety of topics that will include basic zoology, botany and ornithology as well as tracking techniques, species identification skills and how to drive and maintain 4x4 vehicles. Participants will spend plenty of time out in the wilderness, and will come away with a memorable experience and a most worthwhile qualification.

MOREMI KEABETSWE ❱❱

Moremi Keabetswe hails from Lekgophung, a tiny village that lies alongside the private reserve of Madikwe. He belongs to the community of the Balete people, who recently won a land claim on a section of Madikwe. Although he trained as a teacher after leaving school, he was recruited to join the tourism team to head up his community's initiative.

Buffalo Ridge Lodge was opened in November 2004 and Moremi is now the senior guide and assistant manager of the lodge. He is also the chairperson of the Balete Ba Lekgophung Development Trust, which oversees the growth of this venture for the benefit of the approximately 7 000 community members.

Moremi is particularly proud of the fact that Buffalo Ridge is 100 per cent owned by the community, and that within the next few years the community will also take over full management responsibility, including the marketing functions. It's a busy time for him as he juggles his management responsibilities with his real passion, guiding guests around Madikwe.

MURRAY LETCHER »

Although Murray was born and brought up in the shadows of the uKhahlamba/Drakensberg mountain range on the eastern side of South Africa, he has found his home in the dry and harsh flatlands of the Northern Cape.

Murray's formative years in the wilderness were spent in northern KwaZulu-Natal, where he was involved in walking, kayaking and rafting activities and was a dive master at Sodwana Bay. He then joined CC Africa and spent a few years guiding at various lodges in the Sabi Sand and at Phinda, before moving to the Tswalu Kalahari Reserve. He is now the head guide at Tswalu, and is also involved in guide training and several of the reserve's conservation and rehabilitation projects.

For Murray, the inspiration of Tswalu comes from the vast wilderness, being able to guide in a reserve that promotes low-volume ecotourism, and sharing in the owners' vision of rehabilitating the 100 000 ha reserve to its natural state.

« SICELO MBATHA

For Sicelo Mbatha, the wilderness has beckoned since early childhood. Born and brought up in the small village of Hlabisa alongside the Hluhluwe-Imfolozi Game Reserve, Sicelo vividly recalls how the sounds of lions and hyenas in the night stirred his mind. Life as a herd boy also taught him to appreciate the wilds, and later, as a teenager, he took another major step towards his destiny when he was able to visit his father, who was working as a ranger in Imfolozi.

After leaving school, Sicelo pursued his dream by enrolling with Ezemvelo KZN Wildlife as a volunteer. He worked there for three years doing foot patrols, rhino monitoring and general maintenance. His next move came in 2001, when he joined the Wilderness Leadership School, where he is now a senior wilderness guide conducting trails in the Hluhluwe-Imfolozi Game Reserve, iSimangaliso Wetland Park and uKhahlamba/Drakensberg mountains.

He loves Hluhluwe-Imfolozi Game Reserve best. 'The rolling hills, the rhino paths, the bird calls and the silence at night; these are all part of me and this is home for me,' he enthuses.

THULANI ZIKHALE »

Thulani Zikhale has a proud record at Phinda Private Game Reserve: having joined soon after the reserve was established, his 13 years of service make him one of the longest-serving staff members. Born in the town of Hluhluwe, he started his life after school as a barman in a nearby lodge. Shortly thereafter, he heard that Phinda was recruiting and that this was the place to be. His career at the lodge began behind the bar, but soon moved to the kitchen, where he became a chef.

A number of years later, he yearned to try his hand at guiding, and was accepted to undergo the company's guide training course. It was, as he says, 'my best move ever'. Since then he has also acquired his full walking-guide license. Thulani now has eight years' guiding experience and is one of the reserve's senior guides. He spends time at all seven of Phinda's lodges, and is most passionate about the trees and birds of the area.

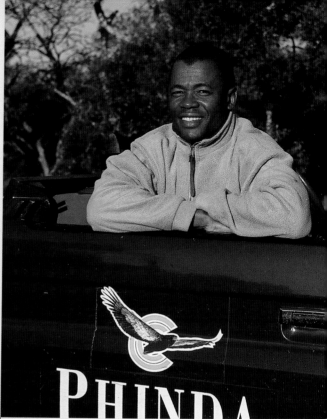

« GODFREY BALOYI

The story of the Makuleke community and the Pafuri concession in the far northern region of the Kruger National Park (KNP) is one of South Africa's most successful land-restitution cases. And Godfrey Baloyi has been involved throughout. He was born in a village on the outskirts of the park to parents who had been removed from Crooks Corner inside the park. After hearing his mother's stories about life on the family's ancestral land, he always yearned to return one day. After leaving school, he qualified as a teacher and spent time teaching in the local community schools.

In 2004, the community was given back its land and Wilderness Safaris became the tourism operator for Pafuri. Godfrey joined the company soon afterwards and helped to build the first lodge on the banks of the Luvuvhu River. He was then chosen to do a guiding training course and qualified as the top student. He has since then become one of the company's top guides. For Godfrey, guiding is an extension of his love for teaching. He wants to help ensure that Pafuri becomes a huge success for the Makuleke community and the KNP.

WILDLIFE
WONDERS

PREVIOUS PAGES *Often overlooked in favour of the large and more glamorous species, the small wonders of the bush are no less impressive, once pointed out.*
LEFT *False Bay is home to one of the largest populations of great white sharks. For viewing experiences from a boat and pelagic birding trips, contact Apex Shark Expeditions at www.apexpredators.com or e-mail sharky1@mweb.co.za*

OPPOSITE TOP *Common waterbuck are found throughout the parks and reserves in the northern regions of South Africa.*

OPPOSITE BOTTOM *South Africa is the only country in which three species of zebra occur. Burchell's zebra, seen here, are the most common and widespread.*

ABOVE *Lion cubs have a high rate of mortality during the first 12 months of life. Starvation and other predators are the biggest killers.*

With less than 150 breeding pairs in the country, the Saddle-billed Stork is listed as endangered. The best chances of seeing these birds are in the Kruger National Park.

The African Penguin is endemic to South Africa and is listed as a threatened species.
The best place to see these birds is at Boulders beach close to Cape Town.

Cheetah are listed as a threatened species on the IUCN Red Data Lists, with the continent-wide population estimated to be approximately 12 000 animals.

The same IUCN Red Data Lists show wild dog as an endangered species. The Kruger National Park and surrounding private reserves have the largest populations in South Africa.

ABOVE *Although leopards are solitary and secretive by nature, sightings of the cat in the Kruger National Park and most of the surrounding private reserves are common. These two sub-adults at play are from Singita Private Game Reserve.*
OPPOSITE *Leopards commonly give birth to one or two cubs, and once habituated, they are particularly curious at a young age.*

The klipspringer, from the family of dwarf antelopes, prefers
a habitat of rocky hillsides and mountain slopes.

Flap-neck chameleons are found in savannah woodlands and feed predominately off insects such as grasshoppers and beetles.

*S*outh Africa has received worldwide acclaim for some of its conservation work, including bringing both the black and white rhino back from the brink of extinction and protecting the great white shark. Its initiatives with transfrontier and corridor conservation and the development of various ecotourism models have also drawn international interest. In addition, numerous biologists and scientists are regarded as being at the top of their respective fields. Despite these achievements, South Africa faces various threats to its wilderness areas and the fauna and flora.

ABOVE *The canned-hunting industry has become a massive blight on South Africa's record of wildlife management. This lion will be auctioned, either to be shot or for breeding stock.*

OPPOSITE *Open-cast mining in the Northern Cape's IAi-IAis/ Richtersveld Transfrontier Park. If left unchecked, activities such as this will become a major cause of habitat destruction.*

Under threat

- A relatively low percentage of South Africa's land enjoys national protection. While the IUCN has set targets of 12 per cent, South Africa has approximately 6.5 per cent of land set aside as parks and reserves. Apart from the Kruger National Park and the Kgalagadi Transfrontier Park, these protected areas are generally small to medium sized, which adds to their vulnerability, especially with regard to biodiversity protection.
- Marine protection is even worse. Although 23 Marine Protected Areas are listed, less than 5 per cent of the coastline and marine resources enjoy national protection. Inadequate funding, inept management and policing, commercial and recreational overfishing, poor mariculture practices and coastal mining are substantial threats to marine biodiversity. Numerous species of fish are threatened or endangered, and abalone stocks are on the brink of collapse due to poaching.
- It is of concern that the standards and will of some of those working for national and provincial wildlife and conservation authorities are questionable. This problem is compounded by poor management and the lack of funds made available to these agencies.
- The succulent Karoo biome is regarded by Conservation International as one of the world's 25 biodiversity hot spots. The region has almost 5 000 plant species, of which almost 2 000 are endemic to the region. Despite this, a mere 2.1 per cent of the region is protected. This biome is the one that will probably suffer most from global warming.
- South Africa has approximately 1 650 plant and weed species listed as alien. These plants are a threat because they change the composition of an ecosystem and outcompete the indigenous species. Many of them spread along water systems, and as a result are a major reason for the depletion of water resources in many areas.
- The Cape Floral Kingdom and its fynbos are particularly threatened by alien and invasive species. Frequent fires, agricultural development and urbanisation are also major threats to fynbos.
- Some breeders of wild animals in South Africa are involved in selective breeding practices such as cross-breeding

and inbreeding. Carried out in order to supply the trophy-hunting industry and those involved in canned hunting, these practices undermine biodiversity protection, and are the beginning of a domestication process.

- Habitat degradation and destruction due to a variety of unsustainable human activities – poaching, deforestation, urbanisation, exploitative commercial developments and slash-and-burn agriculture, for example – threatens biodiversity. Presently, 25 plant and animal species face extinction in the immediate future, while another 38 species face a high risk of extinction in the near future. In total, 15 per cent of plant species, 14 per cent of birds, 24 per cent of reptiles, 18 per cent of amphibians and 37 per cent of mammals are listed as threatened by the IUCN (www.redlist.org).

- Overutilisation of resources is a looming problem in the so-called ecotourism industry. A number of national parks are attracting ever-increasing numbers of visitors, and certain private game reserves, already well developed, continue to allow lodges and tourism infrastructure to be built.

- South Africa has a disproportionately high level of carbon emissions. In 2007, it was ranked nineteenth in the world and was responsible for 1.6 per cent of global emissions. When assessed relative to GDP output, South Africa's global ranking is seventh. It is the largest emitter in Africa, accounting for approximately 40 per cent of the continent's total emissions. This high level of emissions is the result of excessive use of low-grade coal for generating power requirements and inefficient use of power.

- Eskom, the national electricity provider, was rated as the world's second most polluting utility company in 2007 by the Global Development Group. Its annual emissions account for 40.5 per cent of South Africa's total emission of 133 million tons of CO_2. The next worst emitters in the country are Sasol, the oil-from-coal manufacturer, and BHP Billiton, one of the world's largest mining houses.

QUINTON MARTINS »

It's been almost eight years that Quinton Martins, head of the Cape Leopard Trust (CLT), has been roaming the Cederberg mountains in search of leopards. What started out as a quest to determine the population level of the region's threatened apex predator soon developed into a substantial and far-reaching scientific and conservation project that now seems to have become Quinton's life's work.

Born and schooled in the Free Sate, Quinton spent the next few years at university studying law. However, a yearning for a more adventurous and meaningful existence pushed him to take a break. He followed his instincts and headed for the private wildlife reserves of Mpumalanga and the wide open wilderness of northern Botswana, where he worked as a camp manager and guide. An immensely fulfilling period for him, it eventually inspired him to return to university to complete his studies, but this time in zoology. After qualifying, Quinton was soon introduced to the world of research work, with stints studying gorillas in Gabon, researching birds in the Kalahari and teaching research students in the southern Cape.

It was this challenging but appealing work that eventually led to his involvement with the CLT. With a Master's degree in mind, he has widened the focus of the project to include a genetic study and an analysis on the dietary intake of the region's leopards. This will run concurrently with a study on the hyrax population of the Cederberg. His dedication and immense passion have turned the CLT into one South Africa's most successful and high-profile research projects.

Science and conservation

ABOVE *The Eden to Addo mega-hike, which takes place on an annual basis, traverses much of the southern region of the Western Cape and the Eastern Cape.*

South Africa has a substantial number of conservation and scientific agencies in operation. Below is a list that includes some of the larger, more well-known ones.

Biowatch South Africa – This organisation facilitates South Africa's adherence to international and national commitments on biodiversity (www.biowatch.org.za; e-mail: biowatch@mweb.co.za).

BirdLife South Africa – This is South Africa's leading organisation involving anything and everything to do with birds and their survival (www.birdlife.org.za; e-mail: info@birdlife.org.za).

Botanical Society of South Africa – The society contributes to the conservation of the botanical biodiversity in South Africa, with particular focus on the Cape Floral Kingdom and the Succulent Karoo (www.botanicalsociety.org.za; e-mail: info@botanicalsociety.org.za).

Cape Leopard Trust – A study focused on the range, genetic characteristics and behaviour of what is commonly referred to as the Cape mountain leopard. The trust is also involved in strong educational and conservation work (www.capeleopard.org.za; e-mail: capeleopard@hixnet.co.za).

CoastCare – This partnership programme involves the private and public sectors and promotes sustainable coastal development (www.environment.gov.za; e-mail: czm@mcm.wcape.gov.za).

Eden to Addo – An Eastern Cape-based conservation initiative that focuses on the promotion of corridor conservation (www.edentoaddo.co.za).

Endangered Wildlife Trust (EWT) – The organisation focuses on research and conservation projects for threatened and endangered species and ecosystems in southern Africa (www.ewt.org.za; e-mail: ewt@ewt.org.za).

International Fund for Animal Welfare (IFAW) – A global organisation that funds conservation, research and educational projects throughout southern and eastern Africa (www.ifaw.org; Tel: +27 21 424-2086).

Peace Parks Foundation (PPF) – The PPF facilitates the establishment of transfrontier conservation areas (also known as Peace Parks) and offers crucial logistical and financial support to existing projects (www.peaceparks.org; e-mail: parks@ppf.org.za).

South African National Biodiversity Institute (SANBI) – The institute has the responsibility of promoting and protecting the full diversity of South Africa's fauna and flora through planning, research and strategic support programmes at local and international level (www.sanbi.org; e-mail: info@sanbi.org).

The Wilderness Foundation – Linked to The Wilderness Leadership School and with branches in the UK and the USA, this foundation is a conservation organisation focused on educational and experiential projects with the historically disadvantaged citizens of the country. It also aims to influence current and future leaders in acquiring an environmental ethos (www.wildernessfoundation.co.za).

Wildlife and Environment Society of South Africa (WESSA) – Founded in 1926, the society is South Africa's oldest and largest environmental organisation that is non-governmental and membership-based. Through a branch network, WESSA runs numerous programmes that aim to promote participation of the public in conservation (www.wessa.org.za).

WWF South Africa – The World Wide Fund for Nature is one of the world's largest independent organisations dedicated to the conservation of nature. It operates in more than 100 countries and, in South Africa, runs numerous research, educational and policy initiatives (www.panda.org.za; Tel: +27 21 888-2800).

LEFT *A young elephant in the Addo Elephant National Park.*

OUT of the WAY

PREVIOUS PAGES *In the arid semidesert landscapes of the Richtersveld, the kokerboom is the dominant species of tree.* ABOVE *The Orange River, South Africa's largest, forms the international border with Namibia.*

OPPOSITE *Along the northern sections of the west coast, early morning fog from the Atlantic Ocean can penetrate as far as 80 km inland and has a substantial influence on conditions in the Richtersveld region.*

For the intrepid traveller, moving about Africa's most developed country does have certain drawbacks. Continued infrastructural expansion associated with sustained economic growth has meant that those far-flung places that make travelling in many of South Africa's northern neighbours and in certain parts of East Africa so exciting are that much harder to come by in South Africa. In general, the western and northern regions of the Western Cape and most of the Northern Cape offer the remotest destinations in the country, with the IAi-IAis/Richtersveld Transfrontier Park and Tswalu Kalahari Reserve being two of the most rewarding places to visit. Another fascinating 'out of the way' destination is the World Heritage Site, Mapungubwe National Park, situated at the confluence of the Limpopo and Shashe rivers in the far north of Limpopo province. These regions have lower population densities and less infrastructural development than many of South Africa's other regions, making them that much more attractive to travellers seeking to avoid the crowds.

IAi-IAis/Richtersveld Transfrontier Park

The Orange River, in the north, forms South Africa's border with Namibia. As the river courses westwards towards the arid coastline it etches its way through one of South Africa's most remote and desolate national parks. This vast desert terrain is known as the IAi-IAis/Richtersveld Transfrontier Park. Managed jointly by SANParks and the local Nama people, the 160 000 ha of park sweep south from the banks of the river, over rugged hills, cliffs and inaccessible mountain spires. Vast tracts of the park remain untouched. Even the few roads that do wind through this dramatic landscape are accessible only by hardy vehicles with good clearance or 4x4s.

ABOVE *The Korannaberg stretches the full length of the Tswalu Kalahari Reserve in the Northern Cape.*

Seemingly devoid of life, this desert is home to a remarkable range of fauna and flora – some unique to the area. Life-sustaining moisture is delivered by the early morning fog, which rolls in from the cold Atlantic Ocean, a mere 100 km away. Look out for the unusual quiver trees and human-like *halfmens* (half-human). The *halfmens* (*Pachypodium namaquanum*) is revered by the local Nama as the embodiment of their ancestors.

There are three Nama communities on the outskirts of the park. They all live a relatively intact pastoral and seminomadic existence.

There is only one entrance to the South African side of the park, through the Helskloof Gate on the western side. The reception and park offices are an easy half-hour drive away at Sendelingsdrif on the banks of the Orange River.

WHERE TO STAY

There are a number of camps to stay in, which offer either rustic cabins or camping sites with new, well-designed ablution facilities. The heat in summer is a factor to consider when choosing your accommodation – your proximity to the water's edge may make or break your visit. For information on the accommodation options, consult SANParks (www.sanparks.org; e-mail: reservations@sanparks.org).

Tswalu Kalahari Reserve

What Tswalu Kalahari Reserve, the largest privately owned reserve in South Africa, lacks in wildlife density is more than made up for by its wonderfully remote location in the Northern Cape, its low-volume ecotourism footprint, and its well-run conservation programmes.

Tswalu means 'new beginning' in Setswana. The reserve is aptly named; its owners set out in 1999, when they purchased the first tract of farmland, to begin a rehabilitation process that would return much of the region to its natural state. There have been additional purchases since then, and the reserve now covers more than 1 000 sq km of diverse terrain that includes the Korannaberg range running through the centre of the property.

These semi-arid landscapes – dominated by rolling, grass-covered dunes interspersed with sparse scrub and acacia woodlands – are home to various endangered species, including desert-adapted black rhino, roan antelope and wild dog. The reserve also offers great opportunities to view seldom-seen species such as aardvark, aardwolf and the elusive brown hyena.

WHERE TO STAY

Visitors have the choice of two of South Africa's finest lodges, both offering spacious, elegant and refined safari style in tranquil settings. Motse, the main lodge, has eight rooms, while Tarkuni caters for families and groups who prefer the privacy of their own lodge. Activities include game drives, walks and horse riding (www.tswalu.com).

Mapungubwe National Park

This historic and cultural World Heritage Site – proclaimed in 2003 – is a national monument and a national park. While not very difficult to reach, it can be regarded as an out-of-the-way destination because it somehow escapes the attention of most visitors.

Although the region has enjoyed protection status from as far back as 1947, it was officially declared a national park only in 1989. Lying in the far northwestern corner where South Africa's border meets those of Zimbabwe and Botswana, Mapungubwe has more recently also been included as a central component to the greater Limpopo/Shashe Transfrontier Conservation Area.

Historians believe that the stone-walled Iron Age site was a major trading centre and capital for a sophisticated and prosperous society for approximately 300 years, before being abandoned in the fourteenth century. It may also have been a precursor to the kingdom that flourished further north in Great Zimbabwe.

Although a local farmer alerted university archaeologists to the region back in the early 1930s, the racist doctrines of the apartheid era ensured that its historical prominence came to light only after the first democratic elections in 1994. Since the first dig in 1932, a substantial collection of clay, copper, iron, bone, ivory and beadwork has been collected, and various gold-plated artefacts have been unearthed from a number of grave sites.

Besides the archaeological and cultural drawcards, the park offers a variety of other attractions, including good birding, various San rock art sites and the Vhembe Hiking Trail. Lion, elephant and a variety of species of plains game are to be found in the park.

Many of the remains found at various sites in the region are on permanent display in the Old Arts Building of the University of Pretoria (e-mail: mapungubwe@postino.up.ac.za; Tel: +27 12 420-3146).

WHERE TO STAY

For accommodation options, which include self-catering, lodge and camping facilities, consult SANParks (www.sanparks.org; e-mail: reservations@sanparks.org).

BELOW *The hills of Mapungubwe National Park – where an ancient civilisation thrived for almost 300 years between the eleventh and fourteenth centuries.*

the LIFE
and SOUL

South Africa has a remarkable diversity of people covering all colours, creeds and cultures. Kept apart during the apartheid era, the population has only since the early 1990s been thrown together into the melting pot of life. Despite the initial tensions, most citizens are now comfortable with the multicultural nature of South Africa, and although the old racial divisions do still cause discord from time to time, these are now more likely to be along class and ethnic lines. While the country's new political dispensation and upsurge in economic activity have brought many positives, they have also served to hasten the dilution and demise of the traditional cultural lifestyles of the rural population. In their place, new cross-cultural systems are emerging, some of which tend to embrace much of the modern Westernised world. Nevertheless, whether cutting business deals with the hip and moneyed city set, watching a football match amidst the working class or drinking beer with the locals in a country town or rural village, you will find the people warm and welcoming.

PREVIOUS PAGES *Circumcision is still practised by a number of different ethnic groups. These Xhosa initiates are on their way to a ceremony in the Eastern Cape.*

ABOVE *Traditional healers still play a vital role in rural communities throughout South Africa. They dispense everything from herbal medicines to tidings of good fortune.*

Who's who in South Africa

- Of South Africa's 47.9 million people (2007), approximately 37.7 million (79.5 per cent) are of Bantu origin; 4.5 million (9.2 per cent) are white or of European origin; 4.2 million (8.9 per cent) are coloured; and 1.2 million (2.5 per cent) are Indian/Asian.

- Based on the ethno-linguistic distinction, there are four major Bantu-speaking groups in South Africa. The largest group is the Nguni, which comprises the Zulu, Xhosa, Swazi and Ndebele people. The Sotho-Tswana, the Tsonga-Shangaan and the Venda are the other three groups.

- The largest ethnic group is the Zulu people, who traditionally come from KwaZulu-Natal. The next largest groups are the Xhosa people, who traditionally live in the Eastern Cape, and the Tswana people and the Sotho people, who traditionally come from the Highveld regions of South Africa.

- Of the smaller groups, the Ndebele people are traditionally established in central Mpumalanga and the Venda people, who have historical links to the people of Zimbabwe, are traditionally to be found in northern Limpopo. Traditionally, the Tsonga people live along the northern borders of the Kruger National Park, the Swazi people in southern Mpumalanga, and the remnant population of San people in the Northern Cape along the border with Botswana.

- The white people are primarily descended from Dutch, British and French settlers, the first European groups to settle in South Africa. During the 1900s, waves of settlement saw people from various other European countries – most notably Greece, Portugal and Italy – arriving. The white population is spread throughout South Africa.

- The coloured people are descended from the intermarriage of various European settler and local Khoisan groups. The coloured people have formed their own distinctive cultural identity that includes the Griqua and the mostly Muslim Cape Malays. The majority of the coloured population comes from the Western Cape and the Northern Cape.

- The Indian people – primarily Hindu, but there is also a small population of Muslim people – mostly live in and around the city of Durban. Most are descended from the contracted labourers who were brought to work on sugar-cane plantations or came to South Africa as merchants and traders.

- KwaZulu-Natal is home to 21 per cent of South Africa's population. Twenty per cent of the population live in Gauteng and 14.6 per cent live in the Eastern Cape. The Northern Cape, with 2.3 per cent, is the country's least populated province.

- South Africa's Constitution guarantees freedom of worship. Some 80 per cent of South Africans adhere to the Christian faith, 1.5 per cent are Islamic, 1.2 per cent are Hindu and 15 per cent adhere to traditional beliefs or have no religion.

ABOVE *This young girl is from the village of Askham in the Northern Cape.*

In the rural communities of South Africa, people will often have to travel long distances in order to buy food supplies. This group lives along the Wild Coast and has been shopping in Coffee Bay.

This Xhosa woman is smoking a traditional pipe. It is a practice that
is fading as only the older generations still carry out the ritual.

African independent churches

Almost as a form of political protest, headmen, chiefs or groups of elders would lead breakaways from the parent mission church to establish their own congregations. In the process, they sought to maintain some form of independence and authority over their sociocultural systems.

Now known as African independent churches, more than 4 000 of them exist across Africa. Approximately 11 million people – the majority of South Africa's Christian population – belong to these churches. Fuelled in part by the processes of Westernisation and urbanisation, these churches have grown their membership dramatically over the last half century as millions of people have sought to make sense of the ever-changing social and political landscapes in South Africa.

Combining elements of Christianity with traditional African belief systems and customs, many of the independent churches have strong leaders – known as bishops, prophets or messiahs – who become the embodiment of the church. Traditional faith-healing ceremonies, talking in tongues and dancing and drumming are common features of worship in these churches. Based on the characteristics of organisation, worship and teaching, the churches belong to one of four broad streams or groupings: Zionist, Apostolic, Pentecostal and Ethiopian. While most of the churches have substantial memberships, some are small and consist of extended family groups or cater to particular villages only.

With almost five million followers, the Zion Christian Church (ZCC) is the largest of the independent churches in South Africa. Led by charismatic members of the Lekganyane family, it started in the early 1900s after missionaries from the Christian Catholic Apostolic Church of Zion City in Chicago, USA, came to South Africa. Based at Zion City Moria outside Polokwane in Limpopo province, the ZCC draws its membership from across South Africa.

Christianity established a foothold in Africa almost 1900 years ago, but back then it was limited to Ethiopia and parts of northern Africa. It was not until the advent of colonialism and the arrival of Christian missionaries in the 1700s and 1800s that the religion began spreading through southern and eastern Africa. While in some ways successful, the evangelists also experienced resistance as they were regarded as an extension of the colonisation process that sought to dominate all aspects of traditional African life. Many black converts did not accept a complete leap of faith based on the condemnation and destruction of their cultures and customs.

ABOVE *The Zion Christian Church (ZCC) is the largest of the African independent churches in South Africa. These members are on the annual Easter pilgrimage to Zion City Moria in Limpopo province.*

Township life

Townships are a peculiarly South African phenomenon, and have become as quintessentially a part of South Africa's fabric as bushveld safaris, Sunday braais, and football fans' *makaraba*s (sculpted plastic safety hats) and *vuvuzelas* (long plastic trumpets). Most often dusty, underdeveloped and dirty, townships are nonetheless the heartbeat of life for the vast majority of urbanised black South Africans.

Sometimes also known as 'locations' (or *lokasies* in Afrikaans), townships are irrevocably linked to South Africa's racist past. Conceived under the Group Areas Act that outlawed black people and white people living in the same place, townships were designed for the dual purpose of being both dumping grounds for people not classified as white and pools of cheap labour. In order to make police and bureaucratic control easier, apartheid's architects chose the typical grid layout with a single point for entry and exit. They also always set the township a good few kilometres away from the outskirts of every town or city centre, making transport for residents a major hassle. And because townships were designed to remain temporary abodes only, small or dormitory-type dwellings were sanctioned, with little or no provision made for appropriate electricity (Soweto received electricity only in 1988), water and sewage.

While the authorities had some measure of control over the daily lives of black people, they were unable to stem the tide of urbanisation. By the 1970s, the townships were

BELOW *While townships are irrevocably linked to the apartheid era, today they are home for the vast majority of South Africa's poorer urbanised black population.*

growing rapidly as people flocked to the larger towns and cities in search of work. And as the township populations grew, so too did the levels of resentment and protest at the apartheid government's policies. Once the Soweto Riots took hold in 1976, almost every township throughout South Africa became a hotbed of resistance to the government of the day. Most townships still boast that legacy and have a museum or memorial of some sort.

Today most townships are treated either as suburbs or extensions of the main towns or cities. And while some remain underdeveloped and messy, many have enhanced their status and have thriving local economies. In general, while most township dwellers are living below or close to the poverty line, life here remains amazingly vibrant and colourful. The fashion, food, music and even the local township languages all add to the energy so characteristic of South Africa's townships.

SOWETO

The most well known and celebrated of South Africa's townships is Soweto, the sprawling mix of shanty town and formal housing estates that lies approximately 30 km outside Johannesburg in Gauteng. Established in 1932, when the region was first known as Orlando East, it now comprises a collection of once-smaller townships that have merged into a booming metropolis of more than 3.5 million people. It takes its name from the bureaucratic tag of South Western Township, only officially accorded in 1963.

OTHER LARGE TOWNSHIPS

Other well-known large townships worth visiting include Alexandra adjoining Sandton in the northern part of Greater Johannesburg, Atteridgeville outside Pretoria, KwaMashu outside Durban, and Khayelitsha and Guguletu outside Cape Town. Every country town also has a township, and these are more often than not worth visiting.

VISITING TOWNSHIPS

The best way to visit a township is on an official tour with recognised operators. For further information, visit www.saweb.co.za/townships; www.ziboneletours.com; www.vuyaafrica.co.za.

ABOVE *An informal township in the Hex River valley in the Western Cape.*
BELOW *A group of township kids from an informal settlement outside Cape Town.*
OPPOSITE TOP *The Cape Minstrels hold their annual carnival through the streets of Cape Town over the New Year period.*
OPPOSITE BOTTOM *Common features of all townships are murals and graffiti, often bright and humorous, painted on walls and concrete fences.*

So to speak

- South Africa has 11 official languages: Afrikaans, English, isiNdebele, isiXhosa, isiZulu, Sepedi, Sesotho, Setswana, siSwati, Tshivenda and Xitsonga. Of these, only English and Afrikaans are not African-based languages.
- IsiZulu is the most widely spoken language, with almost 24 per cent of people using it as their first language. IsiXhosa (18 per cent) is the second most commonly used language, Afrikaans (13.3 per cent) the third, and Sesotho (9.5 per cent) the fourth.
- Although English (8.2 per cent) is only the fifth most spoken home language, it is the most commonly used language in commercial, public and political life.
- South Africa has a few pidgin languages. Fanagalo has a Zulu base with very simple grammar, but with words from Afrikaans and various other African languages thrown in. Because people from so many different nationalities and tribal groups work in South Africa's mining industry, Fanagalo developed as a universal form of communication between white managers and black labourers. Known as a master—servant relationship type of language, Fanagalo is now discredited because of its association with the apartheid era. Apart from being spoken between the older-generation white and black men, it is seldom heard or spoken these days.
- S'Camto or Isicamtho originally evolved as a form of street slang amongst *tsotsis* (petty criminals). It has a strong Zulu influence, and more recently the younger township generation, including the more educated, has taken to it as a hip way of communicating. A version that is more Afrikaans-based is known as *Tsotsitaal*.

A TRAVELLER'S VOCABULARY

While people in most rural areas will understand you, even if very basically, if you speak English, it is always beneficial to be able, at least, to greet the local people in their own language. Here are some words and phrases that should make your visit more pleasurable.

isiZulu

Hello (to one person) – *Sawubona*
Hello (to more than one person) – *Sanibonani*
How are you? (to one person) – *Unjani?*
How are you? (to more than one person) – *Ninjani?*
What is your name? – *Ungubani?/Ngubani igama lakho?*
Do you speak English? – *Ukhuluma isiNgesi?*
Can you please help me? – *Ungangisiza?*
Thank you – *Ngiyabonga*
Yes – *Yebo/Ehe*
No – *Cha*
Goodbye (to the one going) – *Hamba kahle*
Goodbye (to the one staying) – *Sala kahle*
Please don't steal my car – *Ungayintshontshi/Ngicela ungayebi imoto yami*
No, I don't use drugs – *Cha angizisebenzisi izidakamizwa*
Are Bafana Bafana going to win the World Cup? – *Usho ukuthi aBafanabafana bazakunqoba Indebe Yomhlaba?*

isiXhosa

Hello (to one person) – *Molo*
Hello (to more than one person) – *Molweni*
How are you? (to one person) – *Uphilile na?*
How are you? (to more than one person) – *Ninjani?*
What is your name? – *Ngubani igama lakho?/Ungubani?*
Do you speak English? – *Uyasithetha isiNgisi?*
Can you please help me? – *Ungandinceda?*
Thank you – *Enkosi*
Yes – *Ewe*
No – *Hayi*
Goodbye (to the one going) – *Hamba kakuhle*
Goodbye (to the one staying) – *Sala kakuhle*
Please don't steal my car – *Ungayebi imoto yam*
No, I don't use drugs – *Hayi, andisebenzisi iziyobisi*
Are Bafana Bafana going to win the World Cup? – *Ungathi Abafanabafana baza kuphumelela Indebe Yomhlaba?*

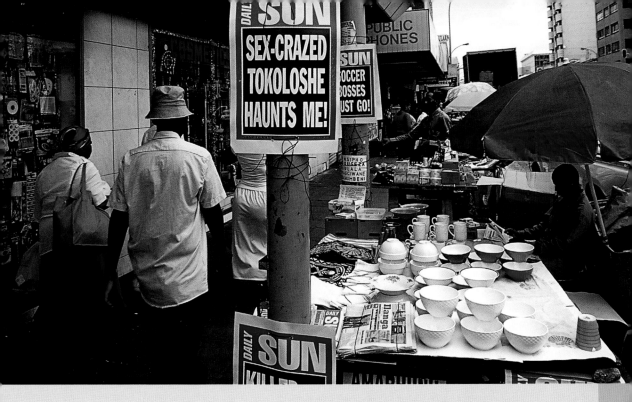

ABOVE *A street market in downtown Durban.*

Afrikaans

Hello (to one person) – *Hallo/Goeiedag*

Hello (to more than one person) – *Hallo/Goeiedag*

How are you? (to one person) – *Hoe gaan dit met jou?*

How are you? (to more than one person) – *Hoe gaan dit met julle?*

What is your name? – *Wat is jou naam?*

Do you speak English? – *Praat jy Engels?*

Can you please help me? – *Kan jy my help, asseblief?*

Thank you – *Dankie*

Yes – *Ja*

No – *Nee*

Goodbye (to the one going) – *Totsiens*

Goodbye (to the one staying) – *Totsiens*

Please don't steal my car – *Asseblief, moenie my motor steel nie*

No, I don't use drugs – *Nee, ek gebruik nie dwelms nie*

Are Bafana Bafana going to win the World Cup? – *Gaan Bafana Bafana die Wêreldbeker wen?*

Sesotho

Hello (to one person) – *Dumela*

Hello (to more than one person) – *Dumelang*

How are you? (to one person) – *O kae*

How are you? (to more than one person) – *Le kae*

What is your name? – *Ke mang? O mang? Lebitso la hao ke mang?*

Do you speak English? – *O bua Sekgowa/Senyesimane*

Can you please help me? – *O tla nthusa? Ke kopa thuso*

Thank you – *Ke a leboga*

Yes – *Ee*

No – *Che*

Goodbye (to the one going) – *Tsamaya hantle*

Goodbye (to the one staying) – *Sala hantle*

Please don't steal my car – *Ka kopo seke wa nkutswetsa koloi yaka*

No, I don't use drugs – *Che, ha ke sebedise dithetefatsi*

Are Bafana Bafana going to win the World Cup? – *Na, Bafanabafana baka hlola dipapading tsa dihlodisano tsa lefatshe na?*

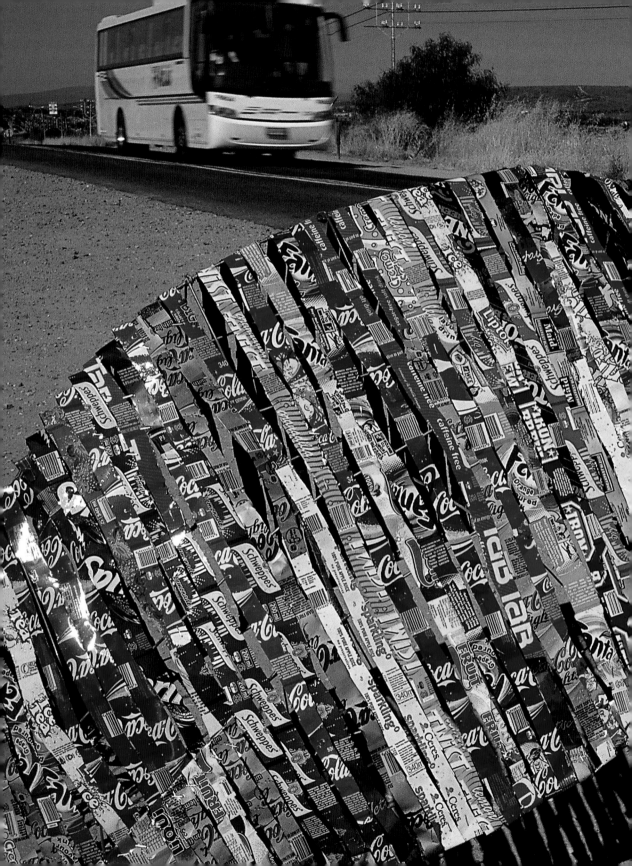

travel ADVISORY

Travel basics))

LOCAL TIME AND DIALLING CODES

Local time

GMT (Greenwich Mean Time) plus 2 hours
European winter time plus 1 hour
United States Eastern Time plus 7 hours
There is no switch to daylight saving.

Dialling codes

The international dialling code for South Africa is +27, followed by an area code and telephone number. The outgoing dialling code is 00 and the Internet code is co.za

WHEN TO TRAVEL

There are two important considerations when choosing your dates: weather and local holiday periods. While South Africa has good conditions for travelling during most of the year, there are three distinct climatic patterns, occurring in different parts of South Africa, of which travellers should be aware (see the Plateaus and Plains chapter).

During the summer end-of-year break (mid-December to mid-January) and the Easter holidays, local tourism levels are at their peak. Cape Town, Durban, popular coastal towns and some national parks are usually packed, making accommodation hard to come by. September and mid-year are also school holiday periods, but are less popular for local travel.

Because of the drier conditions, the peak time for game-viewing is from late July to late October. The summer months are best for bird-watching. Botany enthusiasts tend to want to travel in August and September to catch the magnificent spring flowers in the Western Cape and Namaqualand. For whale-watching, the period of June to November offers the best sightings along the southern and eastern coastline.

VISAS

Visitors from most Commonwealth countries, many western European countries, some African countries and the USA,

PREVIOUS PAGES A curio stall at the roadside outside Oudtshoorn.

Canada, Brazil and Japan, amongst others, are exempt from requiring a holiday or business visa. Travellers from countries that require visas must apply at South African diplomatic representatives abroad. Visitors are entitled to a 90-day stay in South Africa, unless otherwise stated on their visas. Visitors will most often be asked to produce a return air ticket and proof that they have the means to support themselves during their stay. Passports need to be valid for at least six months upon entering and must contain at least two empty pages. (Because these requirements change, it is advisable to check with your travel agent before departing your home country.) When you are in South Africa, you can obtain a visa extension from immigration offices at the Department of Home Affairs.

EMERGENCY SERVICE NUMBERS

Visitors should carry the contact details of their booking agents and ground operators with them at all times as, in the case of an emergency, these numbers may be needed. All local emergency service numbers are carried in the front of local telephone directories. The main national emergency numbers and other related useful numbers are:

Ambulance services – 10177
Police Flying Squad – 10111
Child Line – 080 005-5555
Netcare 911 (24 hr emergency medical assistance) – 082 911
AA emergency line (members only) – 08216111
Emergency if using a cellphone – 112
National Sea Rescue Institute – 082 911 or 021 434-4011
Weather Bureau – 082 162
Local telephone directory enquiries – 1023

HEALTH AND MEDICINE

The northern and eastern regions of South Africa are classified as medium to high risk for malaria. All travellers must consult their local medical practitioner for advice on what malaria prophylaxis to take prior to departure. The only inoculation requirement is a yellow fever vaccination certificate – this is needed only if you enter South Africa within six days of leaving a listed yellow fever country (most countries within central and eastern Africa and some in South America). It is worth consulting your doctor about vaccinations for tetanus, polio, hepatitis A and B, typhoid, rabies and meningitis.

Generally, South Africa has a good to high quality health-care system. Private facilities, although costly, offer excellent treatment and conditions, while government facilities are often overcrowded. All major urban areas and most towns have doctors and Western medicines available, and most larger towns have 24-hour emergency services and extended-hour pharmacies. It is recommended that travellers bring specific medication with them, as prescriptions are required for many drugs. Most hotels, safari lodges and camps have comprehensive medical aid kits on their premises. It is advisable to carry adequate travel insurance that includes emergency evacuation by air.

Tap water in South Africa is drinkable, unless a warning to the contrary is given by your local operator or host. Bottled water is readily available in all hotels, lodges and guesthouses as well as from most stores and restaurants throughout South Africa.

CURRENCY, BANKING AND VAT REFUNDS

Unlike many other African countries, South Africa does not run a dual currency system. South African rand (R), the local currency, is the only cash currency accepted in retail outlets. For exchange purposes, foreign travellers should bring US dollars, British pounds sterling or Euros. Cash is preferable as traveller's cheques are exchanged at lower rates and a number of banks, tourist establishments and retail outlets will not accept them. Major international credit cards (MasterCard and Visa being the most popular) are widely accepted in accommodation units and retail outlets and can be used to withdraw cash at ATMs.

Local banking hours are from 08h30/09h00 to 15h30 Monday to Friday and 09h00 to 11h00 on Saturdays. ATMs operate on a 24-hour basis. They are widely found in all major urban areas and are available in some small towns (see the Safety and Security section overleaf for information on ATM scams).

All non-resident visitors to South Africa are eligible to claim a VAT refund on purchased goods that are being exported within 90 days from date of purchase. Goods must have been purchased at recognised VAT-refund participant stores and claims can be made at most designated exit points, such as international airports, harbours and border posts. Payments will be made only against valid tax invoices for goods exceeding a cost of R250.00, and maximum cheque payments will not exceed R3 000.00. Larger amounts will be processed locally and the refund will be posted. For further information contact the administrator (www.taxrefunds.co.za; e-mail: info@taxrefunds.co.za; Tel: +27 11 394-1117).

INTERNET AND POST OFFICE

At Internet cafés and in accommodation units in major urban areas and towns, Internet facilities are readily available at reasonable rates. Villages in rural areas are unlikely to have access to the Internet.

Urban areas have a number of post offices and most small towns have at least one facility. Hours are from 08h30 to 16h30 Monday to Friday and from 08h00 to 12h00 on Saturdays. Valuables should be posted by registered mail through Postnet, a private mail service available in all major urban areas and many larger towns.

PUBLIC HOLIDAYS

1 January – New Year's Day
21 March – Human Rights Day
March/April – Easter weekend
Easter Monday – Family Day
27 April – Freedom Day
1 May – Workers' Day
16 June – Youth Day
9 August – Women's Day
24 September – Heritage Day
16 December – Day of Reconciliation
25 December – Christmas Day
26 December – Day of Goodwill

ELECTRICITY

All regions in South Africa are supplied with 220–240 volts AC, although lodges in outlying areas may have independent power generators. All plugs and sockets are of the three-pronged, round-pin, 13-amp format and most hotels have 110 volt outlets for electric shavers and other small appliances. Adaptors are available for purchase in city and town stores and for guest use in all hotels and lodges.

In recent years the government has acknowledged that Eskom, the national electricity provider, is struggling to meet the country's electricity demands, and a 'load-shedding' policy has been introduced. Visitors may consequently experience power outages. An upgrading programme has been instituted, which will see Eskom spending R84 bn to add 5 000MW of generation capacity to improve power transmission and distribution networks by 2011.

SAFETY AND SECURITY

Despite crime in South Africa being at unacceptably high levels, tourists are unlikely to be affected if they take sensible precautions. Crime types range from petty theft to armed robbery, car hijacking and rape. The major urban areas, in particular, have high rates of crime in certain areas: commercial and industrial districts, lower-income suburbs and townships, and vacant land.

- Visitors should ensure they get briefed on security by their operators, agents or friends before embarking on activities. Generally, the favoured tourist spots are well patrolled and the daylight hours are the safest.
- Avoid travelling on the Metro train system after dark and don't use unregistered taxis.
- When visiting the townships, use a registered and trusted operator or guide.
- When walking about cities and towns or undertaking a beach or mountain hike close to built-up areas, don't carry valuable jewellery or large amounts of money with you and ensure cellphones and cameras are not conspicuous.
- In the more remote areas, leave beaches, mountains and parks before sunset.
- Do not hitchhike and avoid picking up hitchhikers or giving unknown persons a lift.
- Except for medical emergencies, do not stop to help people along the roadside.
- Be vigilant when using automated teller machines (ATMs) and don't accept any help from strangers, who may be involved in ATM scams. Try to avoid using ATMs at night or when they are situated in quiet areas.

CORRUPTION

Incidents of corruption in South Africa are on the increase. Visitors who are confronted with fraud and corruption at an official level may call the National Anti-Corruption Hotline (Tel: 0800 701701) or visit this website: www.dwaf.gov.za/anticorruption.asp

By reporting such incidents, you will assist in the effort to curb these debilitating practices.

TRAVEL TIPS

- There have been numerous name changes to towns, cities, airports and other geographical features in South Africa over the last decade and a half. If you are on a self-drive trip, it is essential that you carry updated maps reflecting the new names. For more information, go to www.mapstudio.co.za
- Be sure always to carry your travel documents and driver's licence with you as you could be stopped at road blocks and asked to produce them. If your driver's licence includes a photograph of you, then you will not need an international driving licence. Car-rental companies require an international driving licence to be produced upon collection of the car.
- Be aware of speed limits, particularly when passing through towns or built-up areas. There are speed traps and you will be fined if caught speeding.
- Provided that you have not had poor service, tipping is customary in South Africa, with 10 per cent being the guideline for taxis and restaurants. For porters, caddies and tour guides, consult your hotel or tour operator.
- South Africa operates on the metric system.
- Vehicles are driven on the left-hand side of the road.
- Do not attempt to travel without at least two empty pages in your passport. This requirement is strictly monitored and you may be refused entry to South Africa if your passport does not have these.
- Because of the high rates of general crime, it is vitally important for visitors to update themselves on the crime situation in each region they are visiting.

WANT TO READ MORE?

Earth and Life: A Southern African Perspective on a 4.6 Billion-Year Journey by Terence McCarthy and Bruce Rubidge

Ecotravel: South Africa's Top Sites by Philip Harrison

Capturing the Spoor – An Exploration of Southern African Rock Art by Edward and Cathelijne Eastwood

In Celebration of Fynbos by Petra Vandecasteele and Paul Godard

Long Walk to Freedom by Nelson Mandela

Seven Days in Cape Town by Sean Fraser

South Africa Guide by Lonely Planet

Southern African Birdfinder by Callan Cohen, Claire Spottiswoode and Jonathan Rossouw

The Waterberg by William Taylor, Gerald Hinde and David Holt-Biddle

The Wildlife of Southern Africa – A Field Guide to the Animals and Plants of the Region by Vincent Carruthers

The Zulu War – Then and Now by Ian Knight and Ian Castle

THE MUSIC SCENE

South Africa has some brilliant musicians and bands. These are some of the more popular artists. Their music can be bought at most music retail outlets.

- Johnny Clegg and Savuka, Bright Blue, Freshlyground and Mango Groove are the masters of crossover music that

ABOVE *Freshlyground have become world-renowned for their distinctive pop rock sound based on African beats and rhythms.*

mixes pop rock with traditional African beats and rhythms. These bands have achieved international recognition and their music may also be available in stores worldwide.

- The music of Brenda Fassie, Boom Shaka, Mafikizolo, Jabu Khanyile, Simphiwe Dana, Sipho 'Hotstix' Mabuse and Vusi Mahlasela is Afro-pop and folk with strong dance rhythms.
- Hugh Masekela, Miriam Makeba and Dollar Brand (Abdullah Ibrahim) are globally recognised artists known for their jazz-influenced Afrobeat sound.
- Lucky Dube's reggae is internationally known, as is Ladysmith Black Mambazo's mastery of traditional Zulu choral music, while Mahlatini and The Mahotella Queens offer great mbaqanga beats.
- Johannes Kerkorrel and the Gereformeerde Blues Band, Arno Carstens and the Springbok Nude Girls, Just Jinjer (formerly Just Jinger) and Prime Circle are some of South Africa's best rock artists.
- Various compilation sets are certainly worth a spin. Of these, *The Great South African Trip* (Vols 1 and 2) and *The Winds of Change* set are the best. *The African Connection* series compiled by Richard Mwamba is a brilliant collection of music from all over Africa.

Directory))

TOUR AND SAFARI OPERATORS

Invent Africa – www.inventafrica.com; Tel: +27 21 761-7289;
e-mail: reservations@inventafrica.com

Wilderness Safaris – www.wilderness-safaris.com;
Tel: +27 11 807-1800; e-mail: enquiry@wilderness.co.za

CC Africa – www.ccafrica.com; Tel: +27 11 809-4300; e-mail:
information@ccafrica.com

Hunter Hotels – www.hunterhotels.com; Tel: +27 44 532-
7818; e-mail: res@hunterhotels.com

AIRLINES

kulula.com – www.kulula.com; Tel: 0861 585852

1Time – www.1time.co.za

South African Airways – www.flysaa.com; Tel: South Africa
0861 35-9722, USA 0800 722-9675, UK 0870 747-1111,
Germany: 0 69 2998-0320

SA Express – www.flysax.com; Tel: +27 11 978-5577

TRAIN SERVICES

Blue Train – www.bluetrain.co.za; Tel: +27 12 334-8459;
e-mail: info@bluetrain.co.za

Rovos Rail – www.rovos.co.za; Tel: +27 12 315-8242

South African railways – www.spoornet.co.za;
Tel: +27 86 000-8888

CAR RENTAL

Avis – www.avis.co.za; Tel: 0861 11378; e-mail:
reservations@avis.co.za

Budget – www.budget.co.za; Tel: +27 11 398-0123 or
0861 016622

Imperial – www.imperialcarrental.co.za; Tel: +27 11 574-
1000 or 0861 131000

Tempest – www.tempestcarhire.co.za; Tel: +27 11 552-3900

Motorhome Rental South Africa – www.motorhomerental.
co.za

BUS SERVICES

Translux (luxury) – www.translux.co.za; Tel: +27 11 774-
3333 or 0861 589282

City to City (middle) – Details as for Translux

Baz Bus (backpackers) – www.bazbus.com; Tel: +27 21
439-2323

INVESTMENT OPPORTUNITIES

Industrial Development Corporation – www.idc.co.za;
Tel: +27 11 269-3000/3614

Department of Trade and Industry – www.dti.gov.za;
Tel: +27 12 310-9953

**National African Federated Chamber of Commerce and
Industry (NAFCOC)** – www.nafcoc.org.za; Tel: +27 11
268-2800

South African Chamber of Business (SACOB) –
www.sacob.co.za; Tel: +27 11 446-3800

Index

Page numbers in *italics* refer to photographs.

2010 Football World Cup 15

A

aardvark 184
aardwolf 184
abalone 175
Addo Elephant National Park 72, *132–133*, 137, 138, 144, *144–145*, *178–179*
adventure tourism 26, 29–31
IAi-IAis/Richtersveld Transfrontier National Park 24, *38–39*, 45, *71*, 72, 138, *147*, 175, *180–181*, 183–184
air travel 35, 204
Algeria campsite 131
ANC (African National Congress) 58–65
antelope 105, 144, 151, 156
apartheid 13, 16, 23, 25, 31, 49, 51, 52, 53, 54–56, 58, *61*, 62, 64, 65, *65*, 89, 91, 102, 121, 125, 185, 188, 193–194, 196
Apartheid Museum 90
Apex Shark Expeditions *163*
Arniston 109
art galleries 90, *97*, *107*, 117
arts and crafts 35, 37, 86, 90, 97, *107*, 122, *198–199*
Asgisa (Accelerated and Shared Growth Initiative for South Africa) 14, 52
Augrabies Falls National Park 118, 138, 151

B

baboon, chacma 86, *149*, 150, 156
Balgowan 122
banking 201, 202
Barberton 17, 69, 114
Barkly East 45, 123
Barrydale 102
Battlefields Route 34, *54–55*, *56*, 121
Baviaanskloof Wilderness Area 72, 104, 149–150, *150*
Baz Bus 81, 204
Beaufort West 105
Belfast *79*, 114
Berg House and Cottages 123
Bergville 123
Bhangazi Horse Safaris 143, *143*
Biko, Steve 60, 61, 64
biomes 69, *69*, 71, *71*, 72, 79, 144, 148, 175
Biowatch South Africa 177
birding 33–34, *34*, 114, 118, 137

Bird Island 144
Bird Island Nature Reserve 130
BirdLife South Africa 33, 34, 177
birds
  African Broadbill 152
  African Penguin 30, 85, 130, 144, *167*
  Agulhas Clapper Lark 149
  Bearded Vulture 117
  Blue Crane 53, 108
  Botha's Lark 114
  Cape Cormorant 149
  Cape Gannet 130, *131*
  Cape Spurfowl 149
  Cape Sugarbird 149
  Cape Vulture 149, 151, 153
  Common Ostrich *71*, 102, 105, *151*
  cormorant 130
  Hottentot Buttonquail 149
  Knysna Woodpecker 149
  Neergaard's Sunbird 152
  Orange-breasted Sunbird 149
  pelagic birds 33, 86, 137
  Pink-throated Twinspot 152
  Rudd's Apalis 152
  Rudd's Lark 114
  Saddle-billed Stork *166*
  Southern Tchagra 149
  Water Thick-knee *33*
  White-fronted Bee-eater *33*
blesbok 117, 146
Bloemfontein 49, 58, *77*
Bloemhof homestead 106
Blouberg 29
Bloubergstrand 30, 85
Bloukrans Bridge 29
Blue Train 81, *81*, 204
Blyde River Canyon 114, *115*
Bo-Kaap 86, *87*
bontebok 149, 150
Bontebok National Park 138, 150
books 203
Boplaas Cellar 102
Botanical Society of South Africa 177
Botshabelo *37*, 114
Bourke's Luck Potholes 114
Bredasdorp 109
Brenton-on-Sea 110
buffalo 135, *137*, 140, 143, 144, 146, 150, 156
Buffalo Bay 110
Buffalo Ridge Safari Lodge 152, 157
Buffalo River 31
Bulungula Lodge 127
bungee jumping 29
Bushman's Kloof Wilderness Reserve and Retreat 131

bus travel 41, 76, 81, 101, 204
Butterflies for Africa 97

C

Caledon 109
Calitzdorp 27, *98–99*, 102, *103*
Calvinia *66–67*, 107
Camdeboo National Park 106, 138
Camps Bay 29, 30, *32*, 85
Cango Caves 104
canned hunting 137, 140, *174*, 176
Cape Agulhas 70, *70*, 86, 109
Cape Argus/Pick n Pay Cycle Tour 33
Cape Epic 33
Cape Floral Kingdom 24, *25*, 33, 71, 136, 149, 150, 175, 177
Cape Grace hotel 21
Cape Leopard Trust *176*, 177
Cape Minstrels *195*
CapeNature 102, 104, 130, 135, 149
Cape Peninsula 22, 33, 86
Cape Point 22, 86
Cape Point Vineyards 88
Cape St Francis 29, 112
Cape Town
  activities 28, 30, 85–86, 88
  background information 20, 21, 41, *41*, *46–47*, 48, *72*, *84*, 85
  District Six Museum *60*
  Kirstenbosch National Botanical Garden 24, 85–86
  Robben Island 23, *24*, 62, 63, 86
  Table Mountain *20*, 22, 24, 26, 29 30, *41*, *45*, *82–83*, 85, 86, 128
Cape Vidal 141
caracal 149
Carnarvon 107
Carnivore Conservation Group 148
car rental *77*, 202, 204
Cathedral Peak 122
Cathkin Peak 123
Cederberg mountain range 24, 29, *53*, 70, 79, 118, 131, *131*, 176
Ceres 104
chameleon, flap-neck *173*
Champagne Castle 123
Chapman's Peak Drive 33
cheetah *1*, *137*, 148, 152, 156, *168*
Cherry Festival 117
Churchhaven 128
Citrusdal 131
City to City 81, 204
Clanwilliam *79*, 131
Clarens 117, *117*
Cleopatra Mountain Farmhouse *121*, 123

Clifton 29, 85
climate 70, *72–73*, 200
climbing 26, 29, 45, 114, 123, 131
CoastCare 177
Coffee Bay *43*, *124*, *126*, 127–128, *190*
Colchester 144
Colesberg *77*
Comrades Marathon 33
conservation 174–176, *176*, *177*, 179
Constantia Uitsig 89
Constitutional Hill 90
Cradle of Humankind 23, 91, 93
Cradock *107*
Cremorne Estate 128
crime 14, *77*, 90, 202
crocodile 156
Cultural Heartland 114
culture 188, *188*
currency 201

D

Dargle 122
De Bergkant Lodge 104
De Hoop Nature Reserve *25*, 26, *69*, 109, 137, 149
De Krans Cellar 102
De Oude Scholen 107
De Rust *101*, 102, *103*, 104
diamond industry 16–17, 50, 57, 58
Die Hantam Huis 107
Die Hel 104
diving 109, 143
dolphins 30, 112, 137, 144
Doring River 31
Drostdy Hotel 106
Dullstroom 114
Dundee 121
Durban
  activities 28, 29, 33–34, 94, *94*, *96–97*, 97
  background information 73, *77*, 94, *95*, *197*
Durban Art Gallery 97
Durban–Pinetown region 51
Dusi Canoe Marathon 31, 33
Dwesa/Cwebe Nature Reserve 127

E

Eastern Cape 25, 30, 42, 45, 49, 57, *71*, 72, 73, *77*, 104, 105, 111, 122, 123, 137, 144, 146, 156, 158, 177, 189
  coast 26, 29, 124–128
Eastern Cape Parks Board 135, 150

eastern Free State *116*, 117, *117*
East London 34, 49, *77*, 125, 124
Ebenaeser Guest House 80, 119
economy 13–14, 50–52
ecotourism 35, *174*, 176
EcoTraining 157
Eden to Addo Corridor Initiative 26, *177*, 179
education 52
eland 86, 105, 117, 146, 149
Elands Bay 29
electricity 201–202
elephant *21*, *132–133*, 135, *136*, 137, 140, 143, 144, 151, 156, *178–179*, 185
Elephant Coast 34
Elim 109
emergency services 200
Endangered Wildlife Trust (EWT) 148, 179
Estcourt 122
Ezemvelo KwaZulu-Natal Wildlife 135, 158

F

Ficksburg 117
fishing 34, 114, 117, *130*, 143, 175
forests 71, 110, *112*
fossils 23, 53, 91, 93, 105
fox, bat-eared 105
Franschhoek 88, 89
Fraserburg 107
Free State 17, 24, 25, 29, 45, 49, *116*, 117, *117*, 137
Fugard, Athol 107
Fugitive's Drift 121
fynbos 71, *69*, 136

G

Gamkaberg Nature Reserve 102
Gamkaskloof 104
Gansbaai 109, 137
Garden Route
 activities 26, 29, 30
 description 22, 34, 71, *77*, 151
 towns 110, 111, 112, *113*
Gauteng 17, 25, 49–52, *77*, 89, 114, 137, 151, 189, 194
gay and lesbian scene 35, 110
George *77*, 110
Giant's Castle 123, *123*
giraffe *44*, 140, 151
God's Window 114
Goedverwacht 131
Goegap Nature Reserve 79
Golden Gate Highlands National Park *116*, 117, 138
gold industry 16, 17, *17*, 58, 89, 91
Gorah Elephant Camp 144, *144–145*
Gouritz Bridge 29
government 49
Graaff-Reinet 106–107, *107*
Grahamstown 124
grasslands 71, *71*
Greater St Lucia Wetland Park *see* iSimangaliso Wetland Park

Great Escarpment 45, *70*, 71, 72, 122, 123
Great Karoo *10–11*, *66–67*, 70, 72, 104–106, *105*, *106*, *107*
Great Limpopo Transfrontier Park 140
grey rhebok 149
Groot Constantia wine estate 88
guides (wildlife) 157–159, *157*, *158*, *159*

H

halfmens 184
Hamburg 124
Harkerville Forest Trails 30
Harrismith 29
hartebeest, Lichtenstein's 140
hartebeest, red 146, 148, 150
Haute Cabrière Cellar 89
Haven Hotel 127
health 200–201
Hector Pieterson Memorial 61
Hector Pieterson Museum *60*, 91
Hemel and Aarde Valley 109
Hermanus 34, 108, *108*, 137
Hex River Valley 70, *194*
Hidcote 122
Highlands Meander 34, 114
hiking trails
 Cederberg 131
 Dolphin Trail 26
 Eden to Addo mega-hike 26, *177*
 Otter Trail 26, 112, 161
 Oystercatcher Trail 26
 Table Mountain 26
 uKhahlamba/Drakensberg 26, 45
 Vhembe Hiking Trail 185
 Whale Trail *25*, 26, 137, 149
 Wild Coast 26, *127*
 Wilderness Trails 140
Hilton 122
Himeville 123
hippopotamus 30, 143, 156
history 13, *13*, 49, 53–54, 56–61
HIV/AIDS 14, 51–52, *51*
Hluhluwe 143
Hluhluwe-Imfolozi Game Reserve 137, 140–141, *141*, *142*, 158
Hluleka Nature Reserve 127
Hog Hollow 112
Hole-in-the-Wall *124*, 128
horseback safaris 143
Hottentots Holland mountains 108
House Martin 102
Hout Bay 33, 85
Howick 122
Huguenot Tunnel 101
Hunter Hotels 112, 144, 156, 204
Hunter's Country House 112
hyena, brown 137, 148, 158, 184
hyena, spotted 137, 144, *154–155*

I

International Fund for Animal Welfare (IFAW) 179
Internet facilities 201
Invent Africa 204

investment 14, 204
Isandlwana *54–55*, 58, 121
Isibindi Zulu Lodge *120*, 121
iSimangaliso Wetland Park 22, 23, *23*, 30, 141, *143*, 152, 158

J

Jaci's Safari and Tree Lodges 152
Jane Goodall Institute Chimpanzee Sanctuary 114
Jeffreys Bay 29, 112
Johannesburg 14, 17, *17*, 23, 49, 51, *73*, *77*, 89–90, *89*, 90
judiciary 49–50
Jungle Monkey 128

K

Kakamas 80, 119
Kalahari region 34, 70, 118–119, *118*, 119
 see also Kgalagadi Transfrontier National Park
Kalk Bay 85
Kamberg 53
Karoo *40*, 41, 71–72
 see also Great Karoo; Little Karoo
Karoo National Park 105, 138
kayaking 30–31, 143
Kenton on Sea 34, 124
Keurbooms River mouth *4–5*
Kgalagadi Transfrontier Park 45, 118, 135–138, *147*, 148, 175
Kimberley 16, *57*, 77
Kings Camp 152
Kirstenbosch National Botanical Garden 24, 85–86
kite surfing 30, 85
Klaarstroom *40*, 104
Klein Constantia 88
Kleinemonde 124
Klein Karoo Nasionale Kunstefees 102
klipspringer 105, 151, *172*
Kliptown 59
Knysna 30, 33, 110, *111*
Kogelberg Biosphere Reserve 108
kokerboom *180–181*
Korannaberg range 184, *184*
Kosi Bay 141, 143
Kromdraai 23
Kruger House 93
Kruger National Park
 description *21*, 22, 45, 69, 136, 137, 139–140, *139*, 152
 Pafuri region 33
 route from Johannesburg *77*
Kruger, Paul 17, 58
kudu 105, 146, 150
Kwandwe Private Game Reserve 156
KwaZulu-Natal 22, 23, 25, 26, 29–31, 34, 52, *56*, 77, 97, 125, 135, 137, 140, 141, *142*, 152, 189
 KwaZulu-Natal Midlands *120*, 121–122, *121*
 KwaZulu-Natal National Botanical Garden 97

L

Ladismith 102
Lady Grey 123
Ladysmith 121
L'Agulhas 109
Lake St Lucia 141
Lake Sibaya 141
Lambert's Bay 130, *131*
Land's End B&B 110
Langebaan Lagoon 30, 128
language 196–197
Lapalala Wilderness School and Reserve 156
leopard 135, *137*, 140, 144, 149, 150, 156, *170*, *171*, 176, *177*
Lilliput House 117
Limpopo province 25, 29, 49, *51*, 135, 137, 153, 183, 189, 192
Limpopo River 16, 70, 140, 183
Limpopo/Shashe Transfrontier Conservation Area 185
lion *6*, *134*, 135, 137, 140, 144, 148, 152, *154–155*, 156, 158, *165*, *174*, 185
Lion Sands 152
Little Karoo *27*, 34, 70, 101–102, *101*, *103*, 104, *104*, *106*
Llandudno 29, 85
Londolozi 152
Long Tom Pass 114
Lord Milner Hotel *77*
Luvuvhu River 140
lynx 105

M

Machadodorp 114
Madikwe Game Reserve *137*, 152, 157
Magaliesberg 29, 30, 34
Makuleke community 140, 159
Malalane *79*
Mala Mala 152
malaria 200
Maloti mountains 117, *116*, 122
Mandela, Nelson 13, 14, 23, 24, 52, 56, 59–63, *63*, 64, 86, 91, 203
Maphelana 141
Mapungubwe National Park 23, *57*, 138, 183, 185, *185*
Maputaland 143, 152
Marakele National Park 138, 151, 156
Marataba 156
Marine Protected Areas 175
Martins, Helen 107
Martins, Quinton 176, *176*
Mashishing 114
Matjiesfontein *77*, 107
Mbeki, Thabo 13, 61, 63
Meiringspoort 104
Mgeni River 31, 33
Midlands Meander 34, 122
Millard Mountain Lodge 123
Mills, Gus 148, *148*
mining industry 16–17, *16*, *17*, 50, 51, *77*, 89, 114, 175, 176
Mission Rocks 141

Mkhuze 141
Mkomazi River 31
Molteno region 73
Monk's Cowl 123
Montagu 101, 102, 104
Mooi River 122
Mossel Bay 26, 110
mountain biking 30, *31*, 33, 110,
    117, 119
Mountain Club of South Africa 29
Mountain Zebra National Park 137,
    138, 146, *146*
Mpekweni 124
Mpumalanga 25, 29, 34, *36*, 49,
    51, 52, *77*, 114, *115*, 135, 137,
    176, 189
Msunduzi River 33
Mthatha *77*, 127
Muizenberg 29, 30, 85
music scene 203, *203*
Mzimvubu River 128

N

N1 national route *74–75*, 76, *76*, *77*,
    78, 101, 107
N2 national route 29, 76, *77*, 79, 125
N3 national route *77*, *97*, 121
N4 national route *77*, 79
N7 national route 79
N12 national route *77*, 118
N14 national route 80, *80*
Nama communities 24, 119, 183, 184
Namaqualand 44, 79, 118, 128, *128*,
    130, 137, 200
Namibia 79, 30, 80, 118, *182*, 183
Napier 109
Narina Lodge 141
national anthem 53
National Arts Festival 124–125
National Botanical Gardens 93
National Cultural History Museum 93
national flag 52–53
national parks *see* South African
    National Parks
national symbols 53
Nature's Valley 112, 151
Nelson Mandela Bridge *90*
Nelspruit *77*, 79, 114, *114*
Newcastle 121
New England region *42*, *122*, 123
Ngala 152
Nieu-Bethesda 106–107
Noordoewer 118
North Coast 33, 34, *77*, 94
Northern Cape 16, 25, 33, 34, 44, 49,
    72, *73*, 151, 158, 183, *184*, 189
North West 17, 22, 25, 29, 49, 80,
    135, 137, 152
Nottingham Road 122
Nylsvlei 33

O

Oceana Beach and Wildlife Reserve
    124
Ocean View Hotel 128
Old Fort 90

O.R. Tambo International airport *37*, 90
Onseepkans 118
Orange River 16, 30–31, *38–39*, 72,
    73, *79*, 118–119, 151, *182*, 183
oribi 117
oryx 137, *147*, 148, 151
Oudtshoorn 102, 104, *198–199*
Oulap 102
Outeniqua mountains *70*, 102
Overberg 51, *77*, 101, 108–109,
    108, *109*
Owl House 107
Oyster Bay 151
Oyster Festival 110

P

Pafuri Camp 140, 159
Palmiet River 31
Panorama Route 114
paragliding 30
Parker, Dale 156
passports 200, 202
Paternoster *100*, 130
Peace Parks Foundation (PPF) 147,
    179
Pella 80, *80*, 118
peoples
    Basotho people 117
    coloured people 102, 189, *189*
    Indian people 189
    Khoikhoi people 53, 57, 105
    Nama people 119, 184
    Ndebele people *36*, 114, 189
    Nguni people 49, 54, 57, 189
    San people *53*, 105, 189
    Sotho people 54, 57, 189
    Swazi people 54, 57, 189
    Tsonga-Shangaan people 189
    Tswana people 189
    Venda people 189
    white people 189
    Xhosa people 54, 57, 102, 119,
        125, *127*, *186–187*, 189, *190*,
        191
    Zulu people 54, 57, *120*, 121, 189
Phantom Forest Lodge 110
Phinda Private Game Reserve 137,
    158, 152, 159
Pietermaritzburg 33, *97*, 122
Piketberg 79
Pilanesberg Game Reserve 137, 151
Pilgrim's Rest 17, 114
Pink Loerie Mardi Gras 110
Plettenberg Bay *4–5*, *18–19*, *22*, 29,
    30, 44, 110, 112, 137
Plum Tree Lodge 123
Pofadder 80
Port Alfred 124
Port Edward 125
Port Elizabeth 30, 34, 49, 71, *77*, 79,
    110, 124, 144
Porterville 30
Port St Johns 30, *127*, 128
post offices 201
Potberg mountains 149
poverty 14, 52, 90, 194

Pretoria 16, 49, *77*, 81, 85, 92–93, 194
Prince Albert 104, *104*
public holidays 201

Q

quiver tree *66–67*, *180–181*, 184
    see also kokerboom

R

rabbit, riverine 105
Raptor Route 34, 118
Raptor's View 128
Red Mountain *98–99*
Red Mountain Nature Reserve 104
Red Stone Hills 27
religion 189, 192, *192*
rhinoceros, black 105, 135, 137,
    140, 141, 143, 151, 156, 184
rhinoceros, white *124*, 137, 140,
    141, 143, 151, 152, 156, 174
Rhodes 45, 123
Rhodes, Cecil John 58
Richards Bay 34
Richmond *77*
Richtersveld *see IAi-IAis/Richtersveld
    Transfrontier Park*
Riemvasmaak *2–3*, 119
Rietpoort 131
road travel *74–75*, 76–77, *76*,
    79–80, *80*, 202
roan antelope 137, 140, 156, 184
Robben Island 23, *24*, 62, 63, 86
Robberg Nature Reserve *18–19*,
    44, 112
rock art 23, *53*, 53, 105, 122, 131, 185
rock climbing 26, 29, 114, 131
Rocktail Bay 143
Rooiberg Pass 104
Rorke's Drift *56*, 58, 121
Route 62 34, 102
routes 34, *77*, *78*, 79, 80
Rovos Rail 81, 204
Royal Natal National Park 45, 122
Royal Sheba Guesthouse 114
Rustenberg 88

S

Sabie 114
Sabi Sabi 152
Sabi Sand Private Game Reserve 21,
    45, 137, 151–152, *154–155*, 158
sable antelope 137, 140
safety and security 202
St Croix 144
St Francis Bay 34, *111*
St Lucia 143
SALT (Southern African Large
    Telescope) 107
Sammy Marks Museum 93
Sani Pass 123
SANParks *see* South African National
    Parks
Savanna Game Lodge 152
sea kayaking 30
Sederkloof Lodge 150
Sedgefield 110

Sendelingsdrif 184
sharks 86, *97*, 109, *162–163*, 174
Sibuya Game Reserve 124, *125*
Simon's Town 30, 85
Singita Private Game Reserve 140, *170*
Singita Sabi Sand 21
Sisulu, Walter 60, 61, 62
Smuts Museum 93
Sodwana Bay 141, 143
Sophiatown 59
South African National Biodiversity
    Institute (SANBI) 179
South African National Parks
    (SANParks) 25, 85, 135, 138, 139,
    148, 183, 184, 185
South Coast 34, *77*, 94
Southern Cross Beach House B&B
    112
Southernmost Region of Africa
    Route 34
Soweto *12*, 13, 49, 60, 61, 89, 91,
    91, 193, 194
sport 32–33
    see also adventure tourism
springbok (antelope) 53, 105, 117,
    146, 148, 151
Springbok (town) *15*, 79, 80
spring flowers 44, 79, *128*, 130–
    131, 137, 146
Stellenbosch 88, 89
Sterkfontein 23, 91, 93
Sun City 22
Sundays River *70*, 144
Sunshine Coast 34, 124
surfing *28*, 29–30, 85, 94
Sutherland 73, 107
Suurbraak 109
Swartberg Pass 67, 104, *104*
Swartkrans 23
Swartland 79, 131
Swellendam 108, 109

T

Table Mountain 20, 22, 24, 26, 29,
    30, *41*, 45, *82–83*, 85–86
Table Mountain National Park 86, 138
Tambo, Oliver 60, 62
Tanda Tula 152
Tankwa Karoo National Park 138, 151
Tembe Elephant Game Reserve 151
Terroir 89
Tewate Wilderness area 143
Thakadu River Camp 152
Thando's Township Tours 102
threatened species 175–176
Thukela Falls 70, 122
Tiffindell 123
Timbavati Private Nature Reserve 22,
    45, 137, 151–152
Tinga Private Game Lodge 140
Titbits Restaurant *15*
Tokai 30
topography 69–72
tourism offices 25
tour operators 204
Touws River *76*

townships 90, 193–194, *193*, *194*, *195*
township tours 91, 97, 102
train travel 35, 81, *81*, 202, 204
Translux 81, 204
Transvaal Museum 93
travel advisory 200–204
travel tips 35, *37*, 202
TRC (Truth and Reconciliation Commission) 61, 64, 65
Trogon House and Forest Spa 112
Tsala Treetop Lodge 112, *113*
tsessebe 140
Tshwane 92–93
Tsitsikamma National Park 112, *112*, 138, 151
Tswalu Kalahari Reserve 137, 158, 183, 184, *184*
Tulbagh 104, 105
Tulbagh Country Manor Guest House 105
turtle 143
Tutu, Desmond 49, 61, 62, 64, *65*, 91
Two Oceans Aquarium 86
Two Oceans Marathon 32–33

U

uKhahlamba-Drakensberg Park 23, 122
uKhahlamba/Drakensberg range 26, 29, 30, *42*, 45, 54, *70*, *121*, 122–123, *123*, 158

Umngazi River Bungalows and Spa 128
Underberg 123
unemployment 14, 51, 52
Union Buildings *92–93*, 93
Upington 80, 118, 119
uShaka Marine World 94

V

V&A Waterfront *20*, 22, 86
Vaal River 16
vaccinations 201
Valley of Desolation 106
Vanrhynsdorp 79
Van Wyksdorp 104
VAT refunds 201
Velddrif *130*
Vergelegen Estate 88
Victoria Bay 29, 110
Victoria Street market 97
Victoria West 107
Vilakazi Street 91
visas 200
Voortrekker Monument 93
Vredefort Dome 24
Vryburg 80
Vryheid 121

W

Wacky Wine Weekend 101–102
Wakkerstroom 33, 34, 114
Walker, Clive 156

Wartrail New England 123
Waterberg wilderness area *68*, 151, 153, 156
waterbuck *164*
Waterval Boven 29, 79, 114
Wellington 104
West Coast 30, *72*, *100*, 128, *129*, 130, *130*, *131*, *183*
West Coast National Park 128, 138
Western Cape 25, 30, 31, 33, 49, 51, 71, 108, 136, 149, 183, 189, 200
Wetlands Country House & Sheds 114
Whale Route 34
whales 30, 108, 112, *137*, 143, 144, 149, 200
Wheatlands farm 106
white-water rafting 30–31, 118
Wild Card 138–139
Wild Coast 26, 29, 44, *43*, *72–73*, 125, *124*, *126*, *127*, 128, *190*
wild dog 137, 140, *169*, 184
wildebeest, black 117, 146
Wilderness 110
Wilderness Foundation 179
Wilderness Leadership School 141, 142, *142*, 158, 179
Wilderness Safaris 140, 159, 204
Wild Frontier 114
wildlife 136–137
   research projects 148, *176*, 179
   see specific animals

Wildlife and Environment Society of South Africa (WESSA) 179
Willow Historical Guest House *103*, 104
Willowmore *103*, 104
wine industry *12*, 31–32
Wine on the River Festival 102
wine routes
   Breede River winelands 101–102
   Cape Winelands 34, *81*, 86, 88, *88*
   Kakamas and Upington 119
   Little Karoo Wine Route 102
   Walker Bay Wine Route 88
Witwatersrand 17, 58
Wolseley 104
Woody Cape Nature Reserve 124, 144
World Heritage Sites 22–23
Wuppertal 131
WWF South Africa 179

Z

zebra 86, 117, 144
   Burchell's *164*
   Cape mountain 137, 146, *146*, 149, 150
   Hartmann's mountain 105
Zimbabwe 23, 122, 135, 140, 185, 189
Zululand 31
Zuma, Jacob 61
Zuurberg mountains 144

First published in 2009 by Struik Travel & Heritage (an imprint of Random House Struik (Pty) Ltd)
80 McKenzie Street, Cape Town 8001
PO Box 1144, Cape Town, 8000, South Africa

Company Reg. No. 1966/003153/07

www.randomstruik.co.za

Publishers: Felicity Nyikadzino Berold, Claudia Dos Santos
Managing editor: Roelien Theron
Project co-ordinator: Alana Bolligelo
Editor: Patricia Myers Smith
Designer: Pete Bosman
Proofreaders: Mariëlle Renssen, Joy Clack

Reproduction by Hirt & Carter Cape (Pty) Ltd
Printed and bound by Times Offset (M) Sdn Bhd

ISBN 978 1 77007 555 9

Photographic credits
Front cover: Martin Harvey/Images of Africa; half-title page: Robbyn Moir; pp 6, 170, 171 Iva Spitzer; 13 AP Photo/Denis Farrell; 17, 115 Walter Knirr/Images of Africa; 23 Wilderness Safaris; 24, 192 Gallo Images; 25, 32 Jeremy Jowell; 31 Jacques Marais/Images of Africa; 53 (left) Lanz von Hörsten/Images of Africa; 53 (right), 61 (left), 112 Shaen Adey/Images of Africa; 59 Bob Gosani © Bailey's Archives; 63 Gallo Images/Getty Images; 65 AFP/Getty Images; 69, 123 Nigel Dennis/Images of Africa; 81, 167 Hein von Hörsten/Images of Africa; 88 (bottom) Anthony Johnson/Images of Africa; 113, 156 Hunter Hotels; 136, 154–155 Michael McMillan; 142 Wayne Saunders; 143 Richard Daugherty; 148 Gus Mills; 162–163 Chris Fallows/Apexpredators.com; 164 (top & bottom) 166, 173 Peter & Beverly Pickford; 177 Galeo Saintz; 185 Roger de la Harpe/Africaimagery.com; 203 Jonx Pillemer; back cover flap: Russell Juds

Over 50 000 unique African images available to purchase from our image bank at
www.imagesofafrica.co.za